Contents

Mule 2: A Developer's Guide to ESB and Integration Platform

by Peter Delia, and Antoine Borg

ESB. SOA. CXF. JXF. EIP. EAI. These are just a few of the myriad acronyms that make our work harder, not because the subject matter is complex but because the subject matter is vast. What is the real definition of a Service Oriented Architecture (SOA)? Should you perform transformations on an Enterprise Service Bus (ESB) or should that be a service? There are so many things that are not standardized or that are being debated in online forums around the globe.

The thing is, once you've decided that you might need to use an ESB—whether as part of an Enterprise Integration Project (EIP) or as part of a wider SOA initiative, you're faced with a second problem. How do you use it? Vendors are great when it comes to certain types of documentation, but locking yourself into a single vendor's embrace may not be your cup of tea. In the open-source world, while there is a great wealth of documentation available, you need to trawl through wikis, forums, newsgroups, and conferences to get it all.

Our goal when we set out was to take everything we learned while building course materials to teach developers about Mule in the classroom, and make it available in book form. We take a reader who is new to Mule and perhaps ESBs through a series of logical steps starting from basic concepts to building Mule components such as routers and transformers. After reading this book you will be able to write full-blown Mule applications.

Acknowledgements

We'd like to thank all the people who helped make this book possible: Ross Mason, founder of the Mule project and MuleSource for somehow making the time for a thorough technical review; Susan Forshaw, who is helping drive Ricston forward; Wendy Devolder, founder of Skills Matter; and Lisa Hamilton and everyone with Ricston, Apress, and MuleSource that contributed in one way or the other. Last but not least, we hope this book helps readers start to tap the power of Mule!

Chapter 1: Fundamental Mule

This chapter covers the fundamental concepts within Mule, from the definition of an Enterprise Service Bus (ESB) to how you can configure fundamental elements inside Mule to produce a working application.

The Enterprise Service Bus

An Enterprise Service Bus (ESB), sometimes referred to as "messaging middleware," is nothing more than a platform that can carry data between different, disparate applications. Data is carried to and from a series of stops, known as "endpoints," which must be defined for each application. The internals of an ESB contain routing mechanisms that know how to direct specific data from point A to point B.

As you can see from the diagram in Figure 1-1, the ESB is a logical channel that spans your enterprise and each endpoint, and allows data to be sent or received from numerous applications via the bus. Data is transferred to or from each endpoint using a particular protocol—across a TCP connection or perhaps over HTTP, for instance. However, the ESB is more than just the protocols or communication channels; it is the messaging framework.

Mule 2.0 provides this messaging framework rather than the actual middleware required to transfer messages from one endpoint to another. Typically, you could use the Java Message Service (JMS) to transfer data, or perhaps web services, and just use Mule to manage all of this. In fact, Mule does not limit you to using one messaging middleware over another, and it supports 25 different protocols out of the box in the current release. Many more are also available on the community-based MuleForge web site that MuleSource hosts and runs at `http://www.MuleForge.org`.

Figure 1-1. The ESB

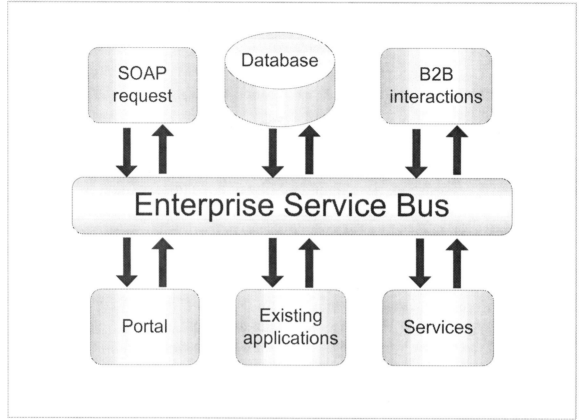

Apart from this messaging, Mule has an object broker that can manage Java objects at runtime. The object broker uses a nonintrusive container that allows you to reuse existing Java objects without the need for additional coding. As well as transferring data to and from other applications, data can also be passed to and from these hosted objects. All this is performed at runtime using the staged event-driven architecture (SEDA) threading model, which was developed by Dr. Matt Walsh.

All thread handling is performed internally within Mule and shielded from the developer. While a lot of items are hidden from view, this is not to suggest that they are inaccessible; you can easily tweak or change anything within Mule by taking advantage of its fully extensible development model. Practically any class within Mule can be replaced or extended to suit your needs.

One subtle advantage of Mule is that it can be used to represent any type of topology merely by reconfiguring it. As illustrated in Figure 1-2, apart from the standard ESB topology you can also set up a peer-to-peer network, client/server, hub-and-spoke, or pipeline model, or you can combine one or more topologies depending on your particular circumstances. Such a combination is then referred to as an Enterprise Service Network (ESN).

Figure 1-2. SOA Topologies

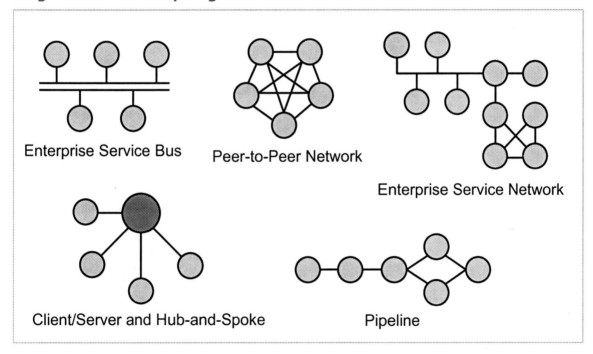

Enterprise Service Bus   Peer-to-Peer Network

Enterprise Service Network

Client/Server and Hub-and-Spoke   Pipeline

Since Mule provides all of this and even adds numerous other features such as security, it is fair to say that it is more than merely an ESB. In fact, the term ESN is frequently used to describe Mule.

Note   This is an important point: Mule does not impose a topology on you or your applications but rather lets you choose the topology that best fits your architecture. This point will be highlighted several times throughout this book. Mule does not impose certain choices on you but instead lets you choose what makes the most architectural sense for your application.

Mule Features

Mule 2.0 provides pluggable connectivity along with a wealth of options out of the box. Common transports such as JMS, HTTP, SMTP, FTP, POP3, and XMPP are all supported natively, as are web services. In some cases, these transports support streaming of large files, but this is dependent on the protocol.[1] Messages transferred through Mule along one of these protocols can behave in any of the following ways:

- Synchronously, meaning a message that is sent needs to generate a reply before the next message can be handled.

- Asynchronously, meaning that multiple messages can be handled before any replies are generated. This is also known as a "fire and forget" pattern.

- In a "request-response" pattern, which is similar to synchronous processing but also allows you to handle the response directly.

---

[1] A full list of transports and the features they support is available on the MuleSource Wiki at http://mule.mulesource.org/x/CwKV.

While data is being transferred through Mule, it can be transformed from one format to another before reaching its destination based on its content, the transports used, or on a series of rules. These routing options can be declared in configuration by the Mule developer or they can be dynamically formed at runtime.

Transactions are supported on specific transports,[2] but both single- and multiple- resource transactions can be used within a Mule application to preserve the state of your data. You can also handle any exceptional situations using Mule's exception strategies, which allow you to catch, route, and handle different errors in different ways.

Remote management of your Mule instances is possible using Java Management Extensions (JMX) technology or by using Mule's internal system notification mechanism. A number of external JMX tools are available that you can use to take full advantage of this, including the MuleHQ product that MuleSource bundles with the Enterprise Edition of Mule.

Enterprise vs. Community Edition

The standard Mule edition that you can freely download (and the version we're referring to in this book) is the Community Edition (CE) originally created by Ross Mason and now still thriving as a popular open source project. Ross has since founded MuleSource, based in San Francisco, which now offers a closed-source Enterprise Edition (EE) of Mule. This is basically the Community Edition with additional QA tools (Galaxy EE, MuleHQ, and Saturn) and subscription support thrown in. However, the

---

[2] The transports that support transactions are documented at http://mule. mulesource.org/display/MULE2USER/Transaction+Management.

release of Mule EE available at the time of writing this book builds on the Mule 1.x line. Ricston offers training and services supporting all versions of Mule.

Here's what the tools that ship with Mule EE offer:

- Saturn is a business-level transaction monitoring tool that allows you to see the state of your business processes while data flows through Mule.
- Galaxy provides a registry and repository for better SOA governance.
- MuleHQ is a web-based interface that allows you to interact with Mule and monitor it remotely using JMX.

Anatomy of a Mule

The configuration format for Mule 2.0 is Spring based, which makes it much more extensible than it was in previous versions. However it is not dependent on Spring; you do not need to install or use Spring if you want to use Mule. The XML namespaces and schemas are provided on the MuleSource site, and because each module is now responsible for its own configuration, there is a separate namespace and schema for each Mule module: one for the core Mule module, one for each of the transports, and so forth.

When launched, Mule looks for a configuration file called `mule-config.xml`, but you can include a file name (and path) to load Mule with a different file of your own.

```
"%MULE_HOME%\bin\mule.bat" -config bin/mule-config.xml
```

Mule can be loaded by running it and using any one of its command-line arguments. The main parameter to use is -config, which allows you to specify a fully-qualified or relative path and file name for the configuration file to use, as shown in the preceding code snippet. Assuming that you have the JDK installed on your computer and that it is configured properly, the single command shown previously will work from within a script. This will launch the wrapper that will, in turn, host Mule. This is the most common method used to launch Mule as a stand-alone application.

Mule can be launched programmatically by using the `org.mule.` `MuleServer` class. This class needs to be created; its constructor accepts a comma-separated list of configuration files that you want to use, as shown here:

```
MuleServer server = new MuleServer ("myConfig.xml,
    myOtherConfig.xml");
server.start (true);
```

Installing Mule as a Service (or Daemon)

Apart from being run in a stand-alone fashion, Mule can also be installed as a service on Windows or as a daemon on Unix.

On Windows, use the `install` parameter shown here:

```
mule install -config myConfig.xml
```

This can be reversed by using the remove command:

```
mule remove
```

Once installed, Mule can be started, stopped, or restarted. In each case, the `config` parameter will accept a comma-separated list of configuration files to use:

```
mule start | restart | stop -config myConfig.xml
```

Additionally, you can use the following Windows `net` command to start and stop Mule:

```
net start | stop mule
```

On Unix you can use the `service` command to start, stop, and restart Mule, but this is only applicable if your operating system supports a SysV-style startup system.

The Design-Time Container

When run, Mule will load its configuration file and host all service components that are declared within it. However, it could just as easily load this information from a third-party container, Spring being the most popular one. You can declare components, classes, and connectors inside a Spring configuration file and load them into Mule by telling Mule which container to use. In fact, you can mix the two; this allows you to add an existing Spring container to your Mule application without having to redeclare all the items.

Tip Other design-time containers are supported too, such as the Pico container and the Hivemind container. These are all available on the MuleForge site.

Mule 2 Configuration File Structure

A typical Mule 2.0 configuration file will contain the following items:

- Connectors need to be declared up front. Having said that, if you are prepared to use a connector with all its default values, you do not need to declare it. Mule will automatically create a connector if one is not explicitly configured.

- Your custom transformers, if any, can be declared and given a name so that you can refer to them by name.

- Global endpoints are also declared beforehand and then referred to by name.

- Lastly, but not least, you should have at least one Mule model available in your application. A Mule model will contain at least one service component that is configured together with its routers, transformers (if any), and endpoints.

The configuration file illustrated here is a perfectly valid Mule configuration file that does absolutely nothing:

```xml
<?xml version="1.0" encoding="UTF-8"?>
<mule xmlns=
    "http://www.mulesource.org/schema/mule/core/2.0"
xmlns:xsi="http://www.w3.org/2001/XMLSchema-instance"
xmlns:spring=
    "http://www.springframework.org/schema/beans"
xsi:schemaLocation=
  "http://www.springframework.org/schema/beans
   http://www.springframework.org/schema/beans/
       spring-beans-2.0.xsd
   http://www.mulesource.org/schema/mule/core/2.0
   http://www.mulesource.org/schema/mule/core/2.0/
       mule.xsd">

   <model name="example"/>

</mule>
```

Note the following items:

- The XML version and encoding are in the first line.

- The opening `<mule>` XML tags contain the references to the XML namespaces and schemas. In this case, the schemas are being loaded from the Web.

- No connectors, transformers, or global endpoints are declared.

- There is a single Mule model called "example," which is empty.

Due to the nature of XML namespaces and their use, Spring items can be declared explicitly inside a Mule configuration file provided that the Spring namespace has been included. Spring beans, or any Spring element, can then be inserted into a Mule configuration file. All Spring XML tags are then prefixed by `<spring...>` and Mule will hand over processing of these items to Spring.

Caution Usage of Spring and Spring elements has changed considerably from previous versions of Mule. Up until Mule 1.4.3, a Spring configuration file could be loaded and parsed by Mule, and all beans defined within it could be used by Mule at runtime by specifying which configuration file to use within `<container-context>` XML tags.

The configuration shown here displays the namespaces required to use Spring inside your Mule configuration. Note that you can also specify Spring beans individually or have a collection of Spring beans included.

```
<?xml version="1.0" encoding="UTF-8"?>
<mule xmlns=
    "http://www.mulesource.org/schema/mule/core/2.0"
xmlns:xsi=http://www.w3.org/2001/XMLSchema-instance
xmlns:beans=
    "http://www.springframework.org/schema/beans"
xsi:schemaLocation=
    "http://www.springframework.org/schema/beans
     http://www.springframework.org/schema/beans/
        springbeans-2.0.xsd
     http://www.mulesource.org/schema/mule/core/
        2.0 METAINF/mule.xsd">

    <!-- Mule config here -->

    <spring:bean>  <!-- ... you can embed Spring
    bean definitions directly ... -->
    </spring:bean>

    <spring:beans> <!-- and you can have nested
    spring defintions -->
    </spring:beans>
</mule>
```

Mule is made up of a large number of different classes and interfaces, but we need to examine these key elements first:

- Service components
- Endpoints
- Connectors
- Routers
- Transformers

Service Components

A service component, historically called a Universal Message Object, is nothing more than a Java object (or a Spring bean) that is hosted and contained by Mule. These components become services within the Mule instance.

Note   The term "Universal Message Object" used to be quite common in Mule 1.x, and you can find it in the online documentation and the source code for Mule 1.x. Starting with Mule 2, this name (and the corresponding acronym UMO) has been removed.

Each component contains some amount of business logic—some code related to the business task that Mule supports. This code does not need to be Mule-specific, as Mule can host components without the need for further coding of your own.

Tip   You can include Mule-specific code should you want to, but this is not obligatory.

Service components will therefore represent key integration logic within your Mule application.

Configuring Service Components

Service components must refer to some kind of Java object, either one of your own or one of the inbuilt objects, which could include the following:

- The **Bridge component**, which bridges the inbound endpoint with the outbound endpoint. This is provided for backward compatibility and is no longer necessary.

- The **Echo component**, which returns whatever it receives.

- The **Log component**, which logs the message (or the message length) in the log files.

Each service is configured using an inbound router collection, a component, and an outbound router collection. If a component is not declared, events are automatically bridged from the inbound endpoints to the outbound endpoints.

The following attributes would be used:

- `name` is a name for this service. This is an attribute for the `<service>` tags.

- `class` is the fully-qualified class name representing this service and is an attribute for the `<component>` tags.

```
<service name="GreeterService">
    <inbound>
        <inbound-endpoint address="http://localhost:8888"
            transformer-refs="HttpRequestToNameString"
            synchronous="true"/>
        <vm:inbound-endpoint path="greeter"
            transformer-refs="StringToNameString"
            synchronous="true"/>
    </inbound>
```

```
Break and indent as:
    <component class=
        "org.mule.samples...
  <outbound>
    <filtering-router>
        <vm:outbound-endpoint path="chitchatter"/>
        <payload-type-filter expectedType=
            "org.mule.samples.hello.NameString"/>
    </filtering-router>
  </outbound>
</service>
```

In this example we have a service called GreeterService that contains the previously used inbound and outbound router collections. The component in use is a custom one so its class name is specified between the router collections.

Endpoints

The Message Endpoint pattern[3] is used in integration projects to answer a simple question: how do you connect an object to a messaging channel? This pattern allows you to connect different applications or objects to a messaging channel. Each protocol (as a messaging channel) is transparently implemented; which means that the component will not know or need to know which protocol is going to be used to send or receive data.

Inside Mule, an endpoint can connect service components to local resources (such as files) or to network resources (for example HTTP connections or third-party applications). They also serve as the location

---

[3] Enterprise Integration Patterns: The Message Endpoint pattern
(http://www.enterpriseintegrationpatterns.com/MessageEndpoint.html)

where a number of other Mule features can be configured, such as filters, transformers, and transactions.

A simple Mule instance is shown in Figure 1-3. Every Mule instance consists of one or more service components that each have one or more endpoints. These endpoints allow data to be received or sent by the service components. Endpoints may be used to connect components together or to connect them to an external application or data source.

Figure 1-3. A Mule Instance

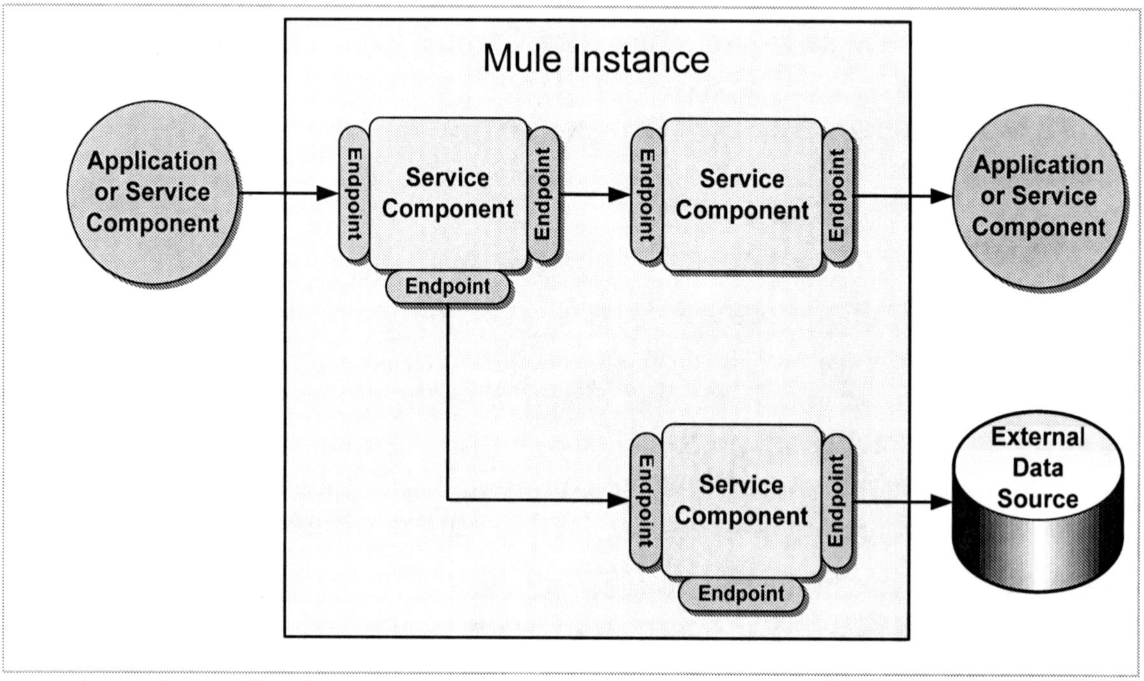

Each Mule application can be made up of one or more Mule instances, so it is possible that service components in separate Mule instances are connected together along an endpoint.

Endpoints can be configured on various Mule elements:

- On the inbound section of a service component. Here the endpoint would be an inbound endpoint and data would be read from it.

- On a router within an outbound section of a service component. Here the endpoint would be an outbound endpoint and data would be written to it.

- In exception strategies, which are used to manage exceptions.

- In catch-all strategies, which are used to manage routing possibilities.

Transports define customized endpoints, which allow for a simpler mechanism to set the address as well as property values. However, the simplest endpoint configuration will only need an address and nothing more. The following attributes are available to all endpoints:

- `synchronous` allows you to specify whether messages read from or written to this endpoint should be read or written synchronously or asynchronously. It defaults to `false` so that all message flows will be asynchronous.

- `connector-ref` lets you specify which connector to use with this transport. You can set up multiple connectors with the same protocol (to connect to multiple JDBC databases, for instance), which lets you tie an endpoint to a specific connector.

- `transformer-ref` lets you specify a comma separated list of transformer names to apply to any messages being written to or read from this endpoint.

```
<inbound-endpoint address="stdio://in"
    transformer-refs="StringToNameString"/>
<outbound-endpoint address="smtp://ross@muleumo.org"/>
```

In the preceding example we can see a single inbound endpoint configured to read from the standard I/O transport's `in` channel (which is the standard input device). It is also configured to use a transformer, `StringToNameString`. In this case, any items read off the console will be converted to `Name` objects before being passed on to the component.

We also have a single outbound endpoint configured to write to an SMTP address.

```
<jms:inbound-endpoint queue="my.queue"/>
<stdio:outbound-endpoint system="OUT"/>
```

In this example we're using transport-specific endpoints rather than the standard ones. We can see that the JMS inbound endpoint has a queue attribute that refers to the name of a JMS queue. The outbound endpoint, on the other hand, has an attribute called `system`, which matches the type of endpoint for the standard I/O transport. The attributes for transport-specific endpoints will vary from one transport to another.

Configuring Global Endpoints

A global endpoint is a named endpoint template that can be declared in the Mule configuration before the Mule model(s). These endpoints can be configured once and then referred to by name from any location that would use endpoints, such as the inbound section of a service or perhaps an exception strategy. You do not need to specify any further transport-specific attributes or properties as everything has already been clearly defined.

Whenever a global endpoint is referenced, a new one will be created for you. You can override the definition of the endpoint at a local level; these changes will not affect any other use of this endpoint and will be specific to this local instance only.

```
<mule>
   <endpoint name="BookingQueue"
       address="vm://my.queue"/>
</mule>
<service>
   <inbound>
      <inbound-endpoint ref="BookingQueue"/>
   </inbound>
         ...
</service>
```

The preceding example shows a global endpoint called `BookingQueue` that refers to a VM queue called `my.queue`. The inbound endpoint section from the previous example has been changed to refer to this endpoint by using the `ref` attribute rather than the `address` attribute. If any different properties were set in the inbound endpoint section, they would not affect any other use of this endpoint. However, any changes in the global endpoint definition would affect all uses of this endpoint.

Connectors

A connector, also known as a provider or a transport, allows a component to send or receive data across a specific protocol. Each protocol is represented inside Mule using a different connector. The connector is a reference to a collection of classes that are responsible for communication, as listed here:

- A **Message Receiver** is a class that knows how to receive raw data using the protocol and convert it into a format that Mule can use.

- A **Message Dispatcher** is a class that knows how to convert Mule data for transmission using the protocol specified.

- A series of optional **transport-specific transformers** allow you to transform the data when being sent or received.

The connector configuration element allows you to specify how a particular protocol is going to behave. For example, you can specify the host name for the SMTP transport or the data source for the JDBC transport. If the default values are sufficient for your needs, you can avoid explicitly declaring a connector, as Mule will construct one on the fly if one is needed but not explicitly declared. Endpoints that use this protocol will automatically be linked to the correct connector.

Each connector element is prefixed with the name of the technology that it describes. Each protocol defines a series of attributes for the connector too; these vary from one protocol to another but one attribute is always available: `name` allows you to assign a name to the connector. You can then refer to this connector by name should you need to. The connector for the standard I/O transport is shown here:

```
<stdio:connector name="SystemStreamConnector"
    promptMessage="Please enter something":
    messageDelayTime="1000"/>
```

The `name` attribute is set to `SystemStreamConnector`, and the following additional attributes are specific to this connector:

- `promptMessage` will be displayed to the user.

- `messageDelayTime` controls how long to wait before displaying the `promptMessage` to the user.

Routers

Based on the Message Router pattern,[4] routers exist to be able to decouple individual processing steps when messages are received from, or are dispatched to, endpoints.

In Mule, inbound routers exist to control messages that are received by an endpoint before the message is passed on to the service component. A message may be filtered or a set of messages may be aggregated before the component is supposed to handle them, for instance. On the outbound side, messages published by the service component are handled by routers before being passed on to the endpoints. These messages may need to be broadcast to multiple endpoints or be split according to specific criteria. A number of routing patterns are available in Mule, and we shall investigate some of the more popular ones.

---

[4]Enterprise Integration Patterns: The Message Router pattern
(http://www.enterpriseintegrationpatterns.com/MessageRouter.html)

The advantage of using routers is that you can have components that focus on the business processing and leave all logic related to routing and routing patterns to these Mule elements.

Note   The service components do not need to do anything else other than perform some specific task, for example validation, without worrying about where the data is coming from or which protocol is used to receive it. The services are therefore loosely coupled from the transports that carry data.

The diagram shown in Figure 1-4 illustrates a single service hosted by Mule. Data read from an endpoint on the left passes through the inbound router(s) configured for the service. The routers hand this message over to the component for processing. Once the component has a return value, it is passed to the outbound routers who, in turn, pass it on to the outbound endpoint, or endpoints.

Figure 1-4. A Single Service in Mule

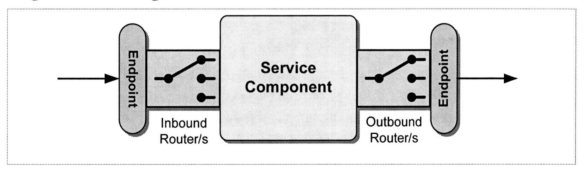

Configuring Routers

Every service component will have both an inbound and outbound router collection so that messages can be read from at least one endpoint and replies can be sent along at least one endpoint.

An inbound router collection will normally have one or more endpoints configured within it. Any messages read from these endpoints will then pass through the default pass-through router that merely hands the message over to the component. Other inbound routing patterns can be used by defining the routers to use after the endpoint(s).

Outbound router collections must be configured using outbound routers, as there is no default router to use. You can define one or more routers and each router would contain the endpoint, or endpoints, required for its operation.

In both cases, if you have more than one router configured in a router collection, you can take advantage of the collection's matchAll attribute. This allows you to determine whether a message should be passed through all the routers, or whether it should be passed through them until one of them handles it.

Implications of matchAll

It is important that you understand how the matchAll router works. For example, assume two Filtering routers are set up such that the first router only accepts items with a value greater than 3, while the second router only accepts items with the name property set to "special:"

- If matchAll is set to false (the default value) as shown on the left-hand side of Figure 1-5, then a message with a value greater than 3 will be accepted, a message whose name property is set to "special" will be accepted, and a message that meets both criteria will also be accepted.

- If `matchAll` is set to `true`, as shown in Figure 1-5 on the right-hand side, then messages that match one of these conditions will be accepted as before, but a message that meets both filters will be accepted twice and processed twice.

Figure 1-5. matchAll = true vs. false

Tip   The `matchAll` attribute is much more suitable for outbound router collections with multiple selection criteria so you can send the same message to multiple destinations based on different criteria.

Inbound Router Collection Example

The following configuration sample defines an inbound router collection with no routers configured on it:

```
<inbound>
    <!-- Incoming HTTP requests -->
    <inbound-endpoint address="http://localhost:8888"
      transformer-refs="HttpRequestToNameString"/>
```

```
<!-- Incoming VM requests -->
<vm:inbound-endpoint path="greeter"
 transformer-refs="StringToNameString"
 synchronous="true"/>
</inbound>
```

There are two inbound endpoints:

- An HTTP endpoint will listen on port 8888 on the localhost for HTTP requests synchronously. The `HttpRequestToNameString` transformer will be used to convert HTTP requests to `NameString` objects before the message is passed to the service component.

- A VM endpoint will listen along the path called "greeter". Any string messages read from this endpoint will be converted to `NameString` objects before being passed to the service component.

Outbound Router Collection Example

The following outbound router collection has three outbound routers configured on it.

```
<outbound>
     <filtering-router>
     <vm:outbound-endpoint path="chitchatter"/>
     <payload-type-filter expectedType=
        "org.mule.samples.hello.NameString"/>
     </filtering-router>
     <filtering-router>
     <vm:outbound-endpoint path="userErrorHandler"/>
     <payload-type-filter expectedType=
        "java.lang.Exception"/>
     </filtering-router>
     <outbound-pass-through-router>
     <stdio:outbound-endpoint system="OUT"/>
     </outbound-pass-through-router>
</outbound>
```

In the first two cases, we're using the filtering outbound router. The first router will pass messages on to the VM channel called "chitchatter," provided that the payload of the message is a `NameString`. If this is not the case, the second router will be invoked, which will pass the message to the `userErrorHandler` VM channel if the payload is a Java exception.

If neither of these conditions is met, the message is handled by the pass-through router, which will output the item to the console's standard output device. If the `matchAll` attribute had been set, then all messages would be passed to the console.

Transformers

The Message Translator pattern[5] allows components to communicate with one another when each component uses different data formats. Mule does not impose a specific message format on you so you can take advantage of whatever format or formats make the most sense for your application.

Three different types of transformers can be used:

- Type transformation involves converting the type of the message, for example converting a byte stream to a string or converting a JMS message to a Java object. The message is untouched but the type will change. Typically, these transformations are transport-specific and are available out of the box.

- Message transformation involves converting the message itself; for example converting a single `BookingRequest` object into a corresponding `AirlineTicket` object. These transformations are very application-specific and would need to be coded intentionally. Mule provides a simple yet

---

[5]Enterprise Integration Patterns: The Message Translator pattern
(`http://www.enterpriseintegrationpatterns.com/`
`MessageTranslator.html`)

powerful framework to chain transformers together for multiple transformations.

- Transformations involving the properties on a message where the message may contain properties, usually related to the transport used. For example, a message sent to an SMTP server would have "To," "From," and "CC" properties.

Transformers must be declared in a Mule configuration before they can be used. They will then be referred to by name, usually from within endpoints.

Each transformer can set the following attributes:

- `name` is a name for the transformer and must be set. The best practice for naming transformers is to be descriptive enough to understand exactly what the transformer does, for example a transformer that converts a byte stream to a string should be named `ByteStreamToString`. When debugging or browsing the configuration it will be immediately obvious what this transformer is supposed to do.

- `returnClass` allows you to specify a different return type to the one that the transformer returns. This is useful for typecasting, for example if your transformer returns a plain `java.lang` object class but you know that it would be a `com.ricstonAirways.AirlineTicket` class, you can specify that the transformer should return `AirlineTicket` objects rather than plain Java objects. Do note that if the data cannot be typecast, this will cause exceptions to be raised. This property is not required.

- `ignoreBadInput` is a flag that allows you to control how a transformer is supposed to react when it receives some sort of data that it was not expecting. If it is set to `true`, any incorrect inbound data will be ignored and passed on to the next transformer (or service). If it is set to `false`, which is the default, any incorrect inbound data will cause an exception to be raised.

Additionally, custom transformers have a `class` attribute that lets you specify the fully-qualified class name for this transformer.

The examples here show two transformers. The first one is for a custom transformer. The second transformer has the `ignoreBadInput` attribute set to `true` and is one of the built-in transformers, `ByteArrayToObject`.

```
<custom-transformer name="StringToNameString"
    class="org.mule.samples.hello.StringToNameString"/>

<byte-array-to-object-transformer
    name="ByteArrayToObject" ignoreBadInput="true"/>
```

Complete Mule 2.0 Configuration File

We can put everything that we've covered so far together to make a usable Mule configuration, as shown here:

```
<mule xmlns=
    "http://www.mulesource.org/schema/mule/core/2.0"
xmlns:xsi=
    "http://www.w3.org/2001/XMLSchema-instance"
xmlns:spring=
    "http://www.springframework.org/schema/beans"
xmlns:http=
    "http://www.mulesource.org/schema/mule/http/2.0"
xmlns:vm=
    "http://www.mulesource.org/schema/mule/vm/2.0"
xsi:schemaLocation=
"http://www.springframework.org/schema/beans
 http://www.springframework.org/schema/beans/
          springbeans-2.0.xsd
 http://www.mulesource.org/schema/mule/core/2.0
 http://www.mulesource.org/schema/mule/core/2.0/mule.xsd
 http://www.mulesource.org/schema/mule/vm/2.0
 http://www.mulesource.org/schema/mule/vm/2.0/
          mule-vm.xsd
 http://www.mulesource.org/schema/mule/http/2.0
 http://www.mulesource.org/schema/mule/http/2.0/
          mulehttp.xsd">
```

```xml
<custom-transformer name="StringToNameString"
  class="org.mule.samples.hello.StringToNameString"/>
<custom-transformer name="HttpRequestToNameString"
  class=
    "org.mule.samples.hello.HttpRequestToNameString"/>

<model name="helloSample">

  <service name="Greeter">

    <inbound>
      <inbound-endpoint
        address="http://localhost:8888"
        transformer-refs="HttpRequestToNameString"
        synchronous="true">
      </inbound-endpoint>
      <vm:inbound-endpoint path="greeter"
        transformer-refs="StringToNameString"
        synchronous="true"/>
    </inbound>

    <component
        class="org.mule.samples.hello.Greeter"/>

    <outbound>
      <filtering-router>
        <vm:outbound-endpoint path="chitchatter"/>
        <payload-type-filter expectedType=
          "org.mule.samples.hello.NameString"/>
      </filtering-router>
      <filtering-router>
        <vm:outbound-endpoint
          path="userErrorHandler"/>
        <payload-type-filter expectedType=
          "java.lang.Exception"/>
      </filtering-router>
    </outbound>
```

```
    </service>

  </model>

 </mule>
```

Here's how it all comes together:

1. First you see the initial namespace and schema declarations as well as the declaration of two transformers.

2. This is followed by the declaration of the model and then a single service component that is called Greeter. The inbound HTTP and VM endpoints are included here.

3. After the inbound router collection, we can see the declaration of the component itself. It points to one of the Mule samples.

4. The outbound router collection follows the component declaration.

The service is complete, as is the model and the entire Mule configuration.

Summary

In summary, while the term ESB normally refers to messaging middleware, Mule extends this definition by adding many other features that it offers as a superset of the functionality offered by an ESB. Also, as you have started to see, Mule does not impose any specific platform or transport on you; it has been designed to work with your existing infrastructure. This is done by making everything pluggable and by having common services available within its central backbone (see Figure 1-6). For these reasons we prefer to think of Mule as an Enterprise Service Network. While Mule can be configured to use the traditional ESB topology, it can also be used for any other topology.

Figure 1-6. The Mule Services Backbone

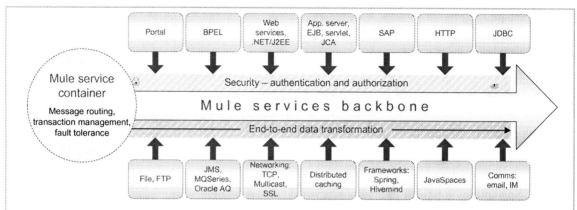

We also took a look at the various Mule elements and the standard integration patterns they are based on. They are all configured inside a Mule configuration file or inside a third-party design-time container, such as Spring. Following are the key elements that make up a Mule configuration file:

- An **XML namespace** that determines the syntax of each XML tag

- The **connectors**, **transformers,** and **global endpoints** that are predeclared and referred to by name from within the Mule model

- **Models** that also contain the service components and their inbound and outbound router collections

- **Properties** that are used to configure any obscure or generic items

Chapter 2: Routers and Routing

The fundamental building blocks in a Mule application are the services that are connected together using routing patterns. Whether you want your data to be passed along from one service to another, or you want a subset of your data to be passed along, or you wish to use a more complex mechanism to decide how data flows along your Enterprise Service Bus, you need to use a router. Knowing what the inbuilt routers can do for you means that you can take full advantage of them—and know what Mule's limitations are.

Note   We'll take a look at how you can extend these routers and create your own in Chapter 7.

Routing Patterns

Three principal types of routing patterns are available in Mule, as shown in Figure 2-1:

- The inbound routers, depicted on the left, accept messages received on endpoints and handle these messages before handing them over to the service component.

- The outbound routers, shown on the right, accept messages received from the service component and handle these messages before handing them over to the outbound endpoints.

- Response routers are used when replies to a previous request need to be handled in some way rather than passing them all on to the originator. Typically these would be used in synchronous situations.

Figure 2-1. Routing Patterns

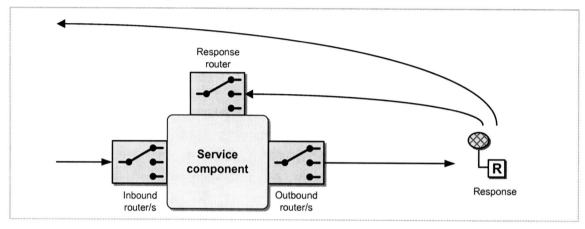

Inbound Routing

Routing patterns used on the inbound side handle messages that are received by a service on one of its inbound endpoints. Because the inbound router may choose to ignore, or drop, the message, not all messages received by the service will be processed by the component.

Any messages received by a service can be either messages that are intended for the service in the first place, or messages that are responses to an original request. The latter will be handled by response routers, which we will talk about later.

Every service in Mule must have an inbound router collection that contains at least one inbound endpoint. You can explicitly declare zero or more inbound routers, but if you do not explicitly declare any, a default inbound pass-through router will automatically be configured by Mule.

Idempotent Routing Pattern

The Idempotent Routing pattern is based on the pattern of the same name to allow a receiver to deal with duplicate messages. This works well in situations where a message will be delivered multiple times but handled only once. For example, in an airport the monitoring software that displays arrivals and departures may receive notification that flight RA1234 has been delayed. This message may be rebroadcast multiple times, but the software only needs to update itself once.

The router will therefore need to know which messages were received and handled already. The default behavior is to persist the unique message ID to disk, although this can be easily extended. Not all protocols support a unique ID; if this is the case the router will raise an exception.

If you don't have unique IDs (or if you'd rather impose idempotency based on other criteria), you can extend the router to note such criteria, for example fields known to be unique within the message.

```
<inbound>
    <!- endpoints listed here -->
    <idempotent-receiver-router
          disablePersistence="true"
          storePath="./idempotent"/>
</inbound>
```

The preceding inbound router configuration is for an idempotent router with the following attributes:

- `disablePersistence` is meant to let Mule know if the list of message IDs can be deleted when Mule is shut down. It defaults to `false`, meaning that the list is persisted. If you set it to `true` and a duplicate message is received after the Mule server was rebooted, the message will be reprocessed.

- `storePath` is the directory that will be used to store the message IDs. The default value for this field is `./.mule/idempotent/`.

On the other hand, the following inbound router configuration shows an inbound idempotent router that will persist the list of message IDs and store them in the default temporary directory:

```
<inbound>
    <!- endpoints listed here -->
    <idempotent-receiver-router/>
</inbound>
```

Selective Consumer Pattern

The Selective Consumer pattern[6] allows a receiver to choose which messages to accept. The ability to ignore certain messages implies the use of some sort of filtering technique. Mule allows for a large number of filters and filter types; these will be described later on in this chapter.

Messages received by an endpoint that are going to be ignored are logged in Mule's log file. This pattern means that while an endpoint will receive x messages, the actual number of messages received by the component will be equal to or less than x.

The filtering performed by this router is applied after the data has been transformed. This can be controlled for cases when you want to filter on the original message received.

```
<inbound>
    <selective-consumer-router
            transformFirst="false">
        <wildcard-filter pattern="Mule*"/>
    </selective-consumer-router>
</inbound>
```

The preceding router illustrates a selective consumer router that is configured to work on the original, untransformed message. By default the transformFirst attribute is set to true. In this example you can see a wildcard filter that will match the payload of the message with the pattern listed. If the payload does not start with the word "Mule", the message will be rejected.

---

[6]Enterprise Integration Patterns: The Selective Consumer pattern
(http://www.enterpriseintegrationpatterns.com/MessageSelector.html)

```
<inbound>
   <selective-consumer-router>
      <payload-type-filter expectedType=
            "com.ricstonairways.messages.Ticket"/>
   </selective-consumer-router>
</inbound>
```

This second router, shown in the preceding code listing, uses a payload type filter and will ignore all messages whose payload is not com.ricstonairways.messages.Ticket.

WireTap Pattern

The WireTap pattern[7] provides the ability to copy messages received on an endpoint to an alternative destination. The message will still be received by the service component (this part of the message flow is not interrupted in any way), but a copy of the message will be sent to an alternative endpoint. There could be another service component on the other side of the endpoint, of course.

The wire tap router in Mule is based on the selective consumer router, so you also have the possibility to filter messages to wire tap a subset of the messages received.

---

[7]Enterprise Integration Patterns: The WireTap pattern
(http://www.enterpriseintegrationpatterns.com/WireTap.html)

```
<inbound>
   <wire-tap-router>
      <payload-type-filter expectedType=
            "com.ricstonairways.messages.Ticket"/>
      <outbound-endpoint address="vm://TappedQueue"/>
   </wire-tap-router>
</inbound>
```

The preceding router is a wire tap inbound router that will forward messages to a VM endpoint called `TappedQueue`. It will only forward messages whose payload is `com.ricstonairways.messages.Ticket`.

```
<inbound>
   <wire-tap-router>
      <outbound-endpoint address="vm://TappedQueue"/>
   </wire-tap-router>
</inbound>
```

This second wire tap router will forward all its messages to the VM endpoint called `TappedQueue`.

The Response Routing Pattern

The Response Routing pattern allows a number of responses to the same request to be put together and handled as one. This is only applicable for synchronous situations, because asynchronous messages do not generate a response. Multiple responses exist because the original message would have been split up by a message splitter router; effectively this means that the router is going to join a number of forked tasks. The function of such a router is to aggregate these messages into one and pass this aggregation back as a response, but it is possible to take other actions, like choosing the most appropriate response.

```
<component ... >
<outbound>
      ...
</outbound>
<async-reply>
```

```
<single-async-reply-router>
    <inbound-endpoint address=
            "jms://flightResponses"/>
    </single-async-reply-router>
</async-reply>
</service>
```

In Mule, the response routers are declared after the `<outbound>` XML tags.

Tip   The response routers handle responses, which makes them usable in synchronous situations. However, as you can see from the previous example, their names contain the word "async".

The response router configured in the preceding example listens for responses on the JMS `flightResponses` queue. The behavior of the single asynchronous reply router is to block the current request thread to wait for a response on an endpoint—so it returns the first response received and ignores all other replies. Thanks to this mechanism you can configure Mule to allow for forking and joining of requests in a single request thread.

Inbound vs. Outbound

The routing patterns that we've seen up until now all work with messages that are received on an endpoint. They're handled by using one or more of the available routing patterns, even if the pattern is a simple one. These messages are handled, queried, inspected, and ultimately routed to the service component if conditions are favorable. There is one key distinction to note between the response routers and a normal inbound router—a response router already knows that the messages it handles are responses, and therefore knows something about them.

On the other side of the equation, we have messages that the services will dispatch. We will handle them in the same way as we handled inbound messages—by applying some sort of routing pattern. The messages will end up on an endpoint of some sort if the conditions are right, but there is no equivalent of a response router in the outbound segment of the message flow; we don't care what sort of message we're sending.

The Chaining Routing Pattern

The Chaining pattern is not based on one of the standard Enterprise Integration Patterns (EIPs). It allows you to synchronously send a message along an endpoint and direct the response to another endpoint without performing any interim processing on the result. You can list any number of endpoints and the message flow will use them sequentially, in the order they are declared.

This is useful for situations where you have a request-response scenario (such as a web service) whose result needs to be directed to another endpoint, for example a JMS queue.

Note that if the message flow is asynchronous, the chaining router will enforce synchronicity on all further message flows until it gets to the last endpoint in its list.

```
<outbound>
   <chaining-router>
      <outbound-endpoint address="tcp://10.0.0.1:815"/>
      <outbound-endpoint address="stdio://OUT"
            transformer-refs="ByteStreamToString"/>
   </chaining-router>
</outbound>
```

The preceding chaining router has two outbound endpoints. The message received from the service component will be sent synchronously to the TCP endpoint and a reply will be expected. This reply will be directed to the next endpoint, which is the console; this endpoint also has a transformer that will convert a byte stream to a string.

Exception-Based Routing Pattern

The Exception-Based pattern is another outbound routing pattern that is not based on Enterprise Integration Patterns. Given a list of endpoints, the router attempts to route the message to the first one in the list; if this fails, it routes the message to the second one, and so on. If all routes fail an exception is raised. This router will override the synchronicity of the endpoint and force the message flow to be synchronous. It needs to do this to ensure that the message route will not fail.

This routing pattern is useful if you have backup routes to the same destination, or if you have alternative routes to take if errors are present:

```
<outbound>
    <exception-based-router>
        <outbound-endpoint address="tcp://10.0.0.1:1234"/>
        <outbound-endpoint address="tcp://10.0.0.2:1234"/>
        <outbound-endpoint address="vm://pendingOrders"/>
    </exception-based-router>
</outbound>
```

This exception-based router has three outbound endpoints. If the first TCP address is unavailable, the message will be routed on to the second IP address. If that too is unavailable, the message will be sent to the VM pendingOrders queue. If this third one fails, an exception will be raised.

The Multicasting Routing Pattern

The Multicasting pattern is also referred to as a broadcast pattern since its aim is to send the same message along multiple endpoints. The router clones the message and sends it on to each endpoint according to the synchronicity declared along that endpoint. These endpoints are listed in any order inside the Mule configuration. Take special care with any transformations, as different transformers may be required—one per endpoint, perhaps.

This pattern is based on the filtering outbound router, so you can filter to make sure only specific messages are broadcast:

```
<outbound>
    <multicasting-router>
        <outbound-endpoint address="tcp://10.0.0.1:1234"
            transformer-refs= "TicketToByteStream"/>
        <outbound-endpoint address="vm://pendingOrders"/>
        <payload-type-filter expectedType=
                  "com.ricstonairways.messages.Ticket"/>
    </multicasting-router>
</outbound>
```

The preceding example shows a multicasting router. It will send the same message to the TCP endpoint as to the VM endpoint, but will need to transform the message before sending it along the TCP endpoint. The router is also configured to filter messages and will only accept `com.ricstonairways.messages.Ticket` objects.

Routing Options

Familiarity with routing patterns is not the only way we can control message routing. We've already seen how selective consumer routers can use filters; this section will talk about the commonly-used filter classes in Mule. We will also discuss the difference between filtering routers and endpoint filtering, how to catch messages that are going to be dropped, and how to configure responses to use response routers.

After reading this section you will be able to create Mule applications that use advanced routing mechanisms to shunt messages around.

Dropping Messages

We saw how some routers choose which messages to process and reject any messages that do not match a filtering condition. These messages are typically "lost," or "dropped," by the router and not handled at all. It is worth looking into the reason for dropped messages though, since such messages could be of significant value—perhaps they imply some sort of error or require additional processing before they can be successfully handled by this service.

In Mule these messages can be caught and handled in one of three ways: the message can be logged, forwarded to a third-party endpoint, or have some sort of customized behavior applied to it.

Catching Dropped Messages

The mechanism to catch these messages is encapsulated inside catch-all-strategy classes. The default ones are as follows:

- `<logging-catch-all-strategy>` logs a copy of the message to the Mule log file before dropping the message.

- `<forwarding-catch-all-strategy>` logs a copy of the message and then forwards it in its entirety to a separate endpoint.

- `<custom-forwarding-catch-all-strategy>` can be extended to provide further processing after having logged and forwarded the message.

- `<custom-catch-all-strategy>` lets you process messages any way you want.

<catch-all-strategy> on Routers

The following example configuration shows an inbound router collection that uses a forwarding catch-all strategy and a selective consumer router. We can see that the router selects messages based on their payload (they must be `com.ricstonairways.Ticket` objects), and if the message is not such an object it is forwarded to the VM `errorQueue`.

```
<inbound>
   <forwarding-catch-all-strategy >
      <outbound-endpoint address="vm://errorQueue"/>
   </forwarding-catch-all-strategy>
   <inbound-endpoint address="vm://newOrders"/>
   <selective-consumer-router>
      <payload-type-filter expectedType=
          "com.ricstonairways.Ticket"/>
   </selective-consumer-router>
</inbound>
```

Filters—By Payload

The `<payload-type-filter>` returns `true` if the Mule message payload matches the expected type, otherwise it returns `false`. If the payload is a class that is a direct descendant of the expected type, the filter will still return `false` because there is no exact match. For example if I am expecting `java.lang.Object` classes and have a message that contains a `com.ricstonairways.Ticket` (where the `Ticket` class inherits from the `Object` class), the filter still returns `false` because it is not a direct match.

The filter works by looking at the payload type, which may or may not be transformed depending on the value of the selective consumer's `transformFirst` attribute. These are the child attributes for this filter:

- `name` should be a unique name that identifies this filter. It makes sense to use a name if the filter is defined globally.

- `not` is a boolean value that inverts the filter condition.

- `expectedType` is the fully-qualified class name of the expected class.

Filters—By Wildcard

The `<wildcard-filter>` matches the string representation of the payload against a pattern using wildcards. The asterisk wildcard is allowed and can be used as follows:

- At the beginning of the pattern to imply that the payload must end with this pattern.
- At the end of the pattern to imply that the payload must start with this pattern.
- On both sides of the pattern to imply that the payload must contain the pattern.

Here are some examples:

- `*name` matches any string that ends with "name"
- `name*` matches any string that starts with "name"
- `*name*` matches any string that contains the word "name"

You can also use multiple patterns by including them as a comma-separated list. The patterns are applied using the OR boolean operator—for example, `*name, *Mule` would match strings ending in "name" or "Mule".

In the following example, any messages read from the VM `newOrders` queue are passed through the selective consumer router and will be accepted, provided that the message contains the word "name" or contains the word "Mule" or ends in "ESB":

```
<inbound>
    <inbound-endpoint address="vm://newOrders"/>
    <selective-consumer-router>
        <wildcard-filter pattern="*name*,*Mule*,*ESB" />
    </selective-consumer-router>
</inbound>
```

Note   The Wildcard filter derives directly from `java.lang.Object` and implements the Filter interface directly. Consequently, it does not have a `not` attribute.

Logical Filters

There are three boolean filters that allow you to perform boolean AND, OR, or NOT operations on filters:

- If you want a message to be accepted only if it matches several filters, you can use the AND filter.

- If you want a message to be accepted only if it matches one of several filters, you can use the OR filter.

- If you want a message to be accepted only if it does not match a specific filter, you can use the NOT filter. (However, this behavior can sometimes be achieved by using the not attribute for each router.)

The router will always see a single filter—whether it is an AND filter that contains several nested filters or not is irrelevant from the router's point of view. You can nest filters as deeply as you need to achieve your conditions, but typically they would not be more than three levels deep.

Take the following configuration code as an example:

```
<inbound>
   <inbound-endpoint address="vm://newOrders"/>
   <selective-consumer-router>
      <and-filter>
         <wildcard-filter pattern=
             "*First*,*Frequent*" not="true"/>
         <payload-type-filter expectedType=
             "com.ricstonairways.Ticket"/>
      </and-filter>
   </selective-consumer-router>
</inbound>
```

The inbound selective consumer router here will accept a message provided that both these conditions are met:

- The message payload does **not** contain the words First or Frequent

- The message payload is com.ricstonairways.Ticket

Here is another example, this time using the OR filter:

```
<inbound>
    <inbound-endpoint address="vm://newOrders"/>
    <selective-consumer-router>
        <or-filter>
            <wildcard-filter pattern=
                    "*First*,*Frequent*" not="true"/>
            <payload-type-filter expectedType=
                    "com.ricstonairways.Ticket"/>
        </or-filter>
    </selective-consumer-router>
</inbound>
```

The inbound selective consumer router here will accept a message provided that one of these conditions is met:

- The message payload does not contain the word First and does not contain the word Frequent

- The message payload is com.ricstonairways.Ticket

The last example is a copy of the previous one and wraps the result of the OR filter with a NOT filter. Note how this is different from having the not attribute enabled for each of the internal filters.

```
<inbound>
    <inbound-endpoint address="vm://newOrders"/>
    <selective-consumer-router>
        <not-filter>
            <or-filter>
                <wildcard-filter pattern=
                        "*First*,*Frequent*" not="true"/>
                <payload-type-filter expectedType=
                        "com.ricstonairways.Ticket"/>
            </or-filter>
        </not-filter>
    </selective-consumer-router>
</inbound>
```

Filters—By Message Property

If you need to filter messages based on the properties rather than the payload, the message property filter is the filter to use. You can list expressions in the form of `name="value"` to specify that you want to look for properties that match a specific value. This is the only way you can filter for meta-information that the underlying transport would provide. By default this filter is case sensitive, but you can turn this off.

The attributes for this filter are as follows:

- `not` reverses the filter expression. By default this is set to `false`. However, this attribute may be dropped, so it would be best to avoid using it.

- `pattern` is the pattern to search for in `name="value"` format.

- `caseSensitive` defaults to `true` and lets you have case-sensitive filtering.

For example consider this configuration:

```
<inbound>
    <inbound-endpoint address="vm://newOrders"/>
    <selective-consumer-router>
        <or-filter>
            <message-property-filter pattern=
                "From=arrivals@ricstonairways.com"/>
            <message-property-filter pattern=
                "From=baggage@ricstonairways.com"/>
        </or-filter>
    </selective-consumer-router>
</inbound>
```

We're using an OR filter to accept messages that match either message property filter. We're looking for messages that have a `From` field that matches the e-mail address for Ricston Airways' Arrivals department or Ricston Airways' Baggage department.

Router Collection Attributes

The only attribute that both inbound and outbound router collections have is the single `matchAll` attribute. By default it is set to `false`. It is used to indicate whether the message should be processed by all routers listed in the collection or whether the first router to accept it should be the only one to process it. Note that if multiple routers handle a message, it may be passed on to the service multiple times.

Routers, unfortunately, cannot be chained and they do not have the boolean operators that filters do. If you need to concatenate routing patterns, you will have to either create a new router or place the routers on individual services (that is, using bridge components) and feed them to one another.

Here is an example config using `matchAll`:

```
<inbound matchAll="true">
    <inbound-endpoint address="vm://newOrders"/>
    <selective-consumer-router>
        <or-filter>
            <message-property-filter pattern=
                "From=heathrow@ricstonairways.com"/>
            <message-property-filter pattern=
                "From=gatwick@ricstonairways.com"/>
        </or-filter>
    </selective-consumer-router>
    <wire-tap-router>
        <outbound-endpoint address="vm://tapped"/>
    </wire-tap-router>
</inbound>
```

Here we have two routers—a selective consumer router and a wire tap router. If the message properties contain a property called `from` that matches either `heathrow@ricstonairways.com` or `gatwick@ricstonairways.com`, then the message will be passed on to the service. The message will also be handed over to the wire tap router, irrespective of the result of the selective consumer router. The wire tap router will pass the message to the service after having sent it to the VM queue called `tapped`.

Redirecting Replies

We saw how responses can be handled by a response router in an earlier chapter and how this router can then aggregate a number of responses together. This can only be done if Mule knows that the response message(s) need to be sent to the endpoint the response router is listening on.

You can configure a `<reply-to>` child element for an outbound router to specify an alternative endpoint that should receive responses, as illustrated in Figure 2-2. This setting will be added to the Mule message as a property and will then be used when the response is going to be generated. All endpoints within a router will use this setting, so this applies for routers that contain multiple endpoints such as splitting routers or multicasting routers.

Figure 2-2. Redirecting Replies to a Response Router

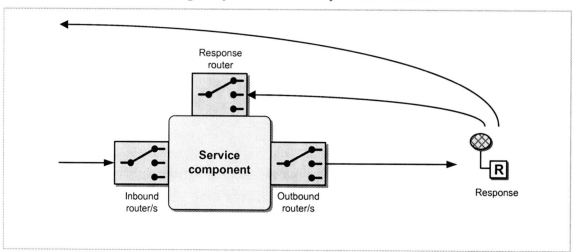

Consider the following example in which the outbound pass-through router sends messages along the `newOrders` VM queue and configures them so that any responses are directed to the VM `responses` queue. The single-async-reply router reads responses off this endpoint and handles them before returning the response to the originator.

```
<outbound>
   <outbound-pass-through-router>
      <vm:outbound-endpoint path="newOrders"/>
      <reply-to address="vm://responses"/>
   </outbound-pass-through-router>
</outbound>
<async-reply>
   <single-async-reply-router>
      <vm:inbound-endpoint path="responses"/>
   </single-async-reply-router>
</async-reply>
```

Summary

The routing patterns shown in this chapter complement the pass-through patterns seen previously. Understanding these patterns allows you to take advantage of the flexibility Mule delivers without having to code (or re-code) this sort of logic within your services. You also saw the wide range of options available for routing as well as filtering possibilities.

All these allow Mule to route your data to and from the various services for you through a powerful and easily extensible series of interfaces—all done via configuration.

Chapter 3: Modeling Applications

Knowledge of the individual Mule elements means that you can start thinking in terms of services, routers, endpoints, and transformers. When you prepare to develop an application, however, it may not be obvious what should be a service or a router or a transformer. In this chapter we are going to explore a case study and model it using Mule. By the end of this chapter you will be able to model applications using Mule.

Real-World Scenario

Ricston Airways is an airline that operates daily flights from a single airport. The procedure to check in a passenger at this airport is as follows:

1. The airline's back-end system is queried to ensure that the passenger who wants to check in actually has a ticket.

2. If one was not already reserved, a seat is allocated to the passenger. While preferences like aisle or window seats are taken into consideration, an expert system tries to balance the aircraft and then allocates a seat.

3. The weight of the passenger's luggage is calculated through the integrated scale at the check-in counter. Luggage information is sent to the luggage tag printer hooked up at the counter. These tags are placed on the bags and a receipt is given to the passenger.

4. The airport is then queried for information about the flight—usually just the gate number.

5. All necessary boarding information is then printed on a boarding card that may vary from one airport to another, but that will always contain the passenger's name, flight details, seat number, gate number, and boarding time.

The information collected is then stored with the original passenger record and used by the airline later.

Checking In

Every check-in counter needs suitable software to manage the entire check-in process. This software must be able to interact with various other systems and access the correct information to complete the process. This airport is replacing its aging system to use new Java-based software that can integrate with the existing framework.

A passenger checks in by producing proof of identity and proof that he holds a valid ticket. Proof of identity allows check-in staff to verify the person's name (which should be on the ticket). Proof of a ticket is a valid Passenger Name Record (PNR). The airline's database back end is queried with these two pieces of information and, if verified, returns the details about this passenger and his booking. The database is stored remotely at the airline's headquarters, so this would be a web service call. If the PNR is not found, or if the PNR and passenger name do not match, check-in cannot be completed.

When all information about the booking is available, check-in staff can see if a seat was preselected or not. If one was preselected this step is complete, but if not, the airline's expert system will select a seat for the passenger. The passenger may have seat preferences (window or aisle); however, if the preferred seat is not available, the passenger will have to accept whatever the expert system allocates.

The expert system is also remote, and therefore communication at this stage also occurs via web services.

Luggage Handling

Once a seat is allocated, check-in staff can focus on the passenger's luggage. Each check-in counter is equipped with a scale that, when queried, sends its current reading over a TCP connection. This is done for each piece of luggage. An existing Java service—the BoardingCard service—knows how to interact with the scale.

These luggage details are collected by the check-in software and returned to the counter's onboard electronics; the appropriate luggage tags are then printed. It is the check-in staff's responsibility to manually affix these tags to the luggage. Receipts are given to the passenger so they can claim the luggage at their destination.

Airport Interaction

The airport is the only entity that knows which gate a flight is going to board from; this information can change at any time. Consequently, the gate number for a flight cannot be cached, but must be requeried every time. Gate number requests are made using web service calls. The existing `BoardingCard` service can also interact with the airport to retrieve the gate details.

All of this information is put together to produce the boarding card required by the passenger to board his flight. This information is also sent back to the airline to be stored for later use.

Modeling the Solution

Our task for this session is to model the given example using Mule and the various Mule elements to demonstrate how all of these system requirements can be integrated.

Confirming Passenger Details

The first step is to verify passenger details. We know that a web service call will be made to the airline, but we also know that without the passenger details the check-in process cannot continue. Initially, the PNR and passenger name are obtained and entered manually by the check-in staff. The system should send this information to the airline via the appropriate web service. The airline will respond with the passenger's details, as shown in Figure 3-1.

Figure 3-1. Confirming Passenger Details

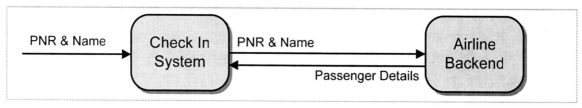

Note   The scenario represented in Figure 3-1 is a request-response; we need to wait for the web service to finish processing and return a result.

Allocating a Seat

Figure 3-2 illustrates how, once we have the passenger details, we can see if a seat is allocated and, if not, the expert system can be queried for a seat.

Figure 3-2. Allocating a Seat to a Passenger

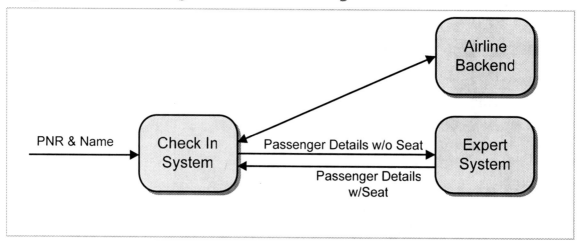

Weighing the Luggage

Once the seat is allocated we pass the full passenger details to the `BoardingCard` service, which is designed to interact with the scale built in to the check-in counter. As you can see in Figure 3-3, this connection is made from within the BoardingCard service.

Figure 3-3. Weighing the Luggage

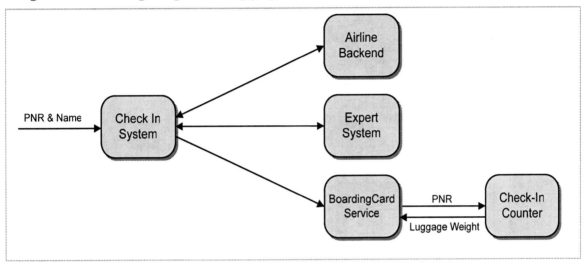

Retrieving the Gate Number

The BoardingCard service also knows how to communicate with the airport and retrieve the gate number for a given flight. The BoardingCard service is still in control of the message flow at this stage; note in Figure 3-4 how it has yet to produce an output.

Figure 3-4. Retrieving the Gate Number

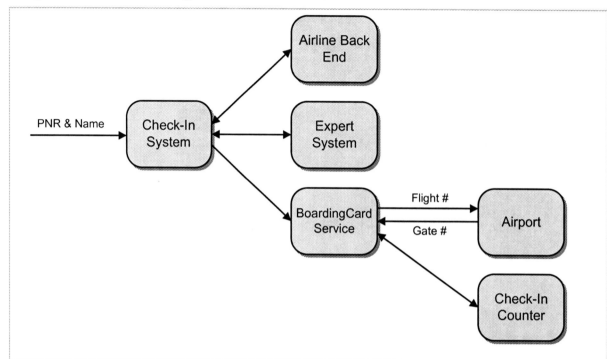

Producing a Boarding Card

The last step is to produce a boarding card (see Figure 3-5). This information is sent to the check-in counter staff, who knows how to print a valid boarding card for the passenger. Additionally, the completed passenger details are passed back to the airline to maintain records.

Figure 3-5. Producing a Boarding Card

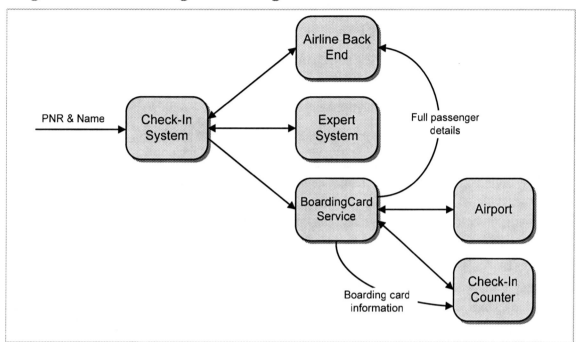

Modeling Points

We can see from this modeled example that Mule can interact directly with external applications, provided it can use an endpoint that the third-party application understands. While modeling the application, we can consider any third-party items as services that Mule will use. Other services will be Mule-hosted components that form part of the entire integration project.

As you may have noticed, the individual steps that make up the entire process are represented by services. The routing and transformation of data, if any, was not shown in this example. The best practice is to let Mule handle the routing and transformation of data rather than the services; the identification of the routing patterns and transformation requirements has been ignored up to this point.

Implementing a Modeled Application

Implementing this modeled example will involve the following activities:

1. Coding the services and any other required classes. All of these items should be tested properly before being used inside Mule.

2. Identifying the correct routing patterns needed.

3. Identifying any locations where transformations are required.

4. Building the Mule configuration using these services. The best practice is to test the routing logic first, and independently of the transports that will be used. You can achieve this by using virtual channels (the VM transport) to connect the services to one another, which frees you to focus on the correct choice of routing pattern and transformation without the overhead or potential problems that live transports may introduce.

5. The Mule configuration needs to be thoroughly tested to ensure that the routing logic does what it is supposed to do. This can be achieved using Mule-oriented Junit tests—a topic that is covered in the next chapter.

6. When all tests pass successfully, you can start introducing the live transports.

Summary

Modeling applications in Mule involves thinking about the different steps that need to be taken for the individual services Mule will host or interact with. Routers govern how the data will flow from one service to another, and transformers are needed to convert data from one format to another.

The Mule application can be built from such a model by using VM channels initially, to let you focus on the routing logic; you can replace these endpoints with the live transports when you are satisfied that the routing has been implemented properly.

Chapter 4: Creating a Mule Application

In the previous chapter we explored a case study and learned how to model it in Mule. In this chapter we'll look at how to go about implementing and testing your model. For those of you who have already downloaded and installed Mule, you may want to skip the next section and go directly to "The Mule IDE."

Core Tools and Components

To start with you'll need to have the following, at minimum:

- A Java platform: Anything that runs JDK 1.5 or higher available from http://java.sun.com/javaee/downloads/index.jsp.

- A Mule distribution: Get the latest one from `http://mule.mulesource.org/ display/MULE/Download`.

- An IDE: Eclipse or IntelliJ are two popular choices.

Note   All references to an IDE in this book refer to the Eclipse IDE.

Installing Mule

First you should download the Mule distribution and unpack it to your hard disk. Next read `INSTALL.txt` in the root of the Mule distribution and visit `http://www.mulesource.org/display/MULE2INTRO/Installing+Mu le` to get your environment set up correctly. Of course if you don't have a Java runtime or SDK installed you'll need to do that from the Sun site. In addition to this it is important to define an environment variable, `MULE_HOME`, which specifies the path to the Mule distribution.

Finally, for application development you'll need to set up an IDE. We refer to Eclipse in this book but you can work with the environment of your choice.

The Mule IDE

An IDE project for Mule (separate from the core Mule project) is available as an Eclipse plug-in from the MuleForge site. At the time of this writing, a developer milestone was available for it but was not yet complete. The Mule IDE is designed for Eclipse Europa and depends on the Eclipse Modeling Framework (EMF) and the Graphical Editing Framework (GEF), both of which are available from the main Eclipse site.

Tip   You can find the Mule IDE on the MuleForge site at `http://www.mulesource.org/display/MULEIDE/Home`.

The intention is to have a fully visual, drag-and-drop interface that will allow you to build Mule applications without needing to delve into the configuration itself. At the moment this feature is not yet available. Currently you can use the IDE to view your services graphically on a "services" page (see Figure 4-1), which appears as a separate page within any Mule XML configuration file and is accessed from the Services tab. This page lets you view the services one by one and inspect the properties of the various elements that make up a service. You can modify these properties by double-clicking elements or right-clicking and selecting "Show Properties View". A "properties" page then displays below the services view listing properties that may be edited.

You can also use the IDE to view global settings for the Mule project on an "overview" page that lets you define which namespaces to use, what global endpoints you may have, a list of connectors, a list of transformers, and a list of globally-available filters.

Figure 4-1. The Mule IDE services view

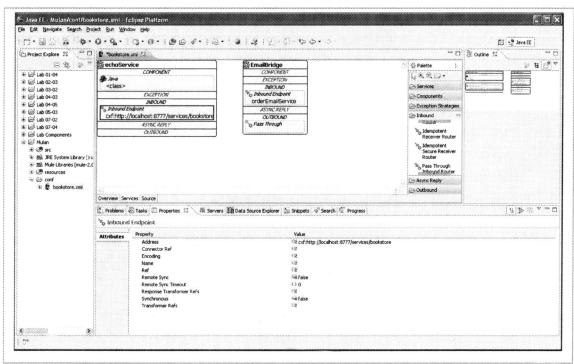

By the time you read this, additional features may be available. Until the IDE reaches GA (General Availability), we recommend you evaluate it, but do not expect to be able to make it part of your day-to-day toolkit for Mule development.

Creating Your Mule Application

Once you have your tools and components in place and configured, creating and running a Mule application is quite straightforward.

Service Components

For starters you will need to put the POJOs (Plain Old Java Objects) and/or beans that you intend to use in your application in place. This might be as simple as copying them over from some other project or location, or you might need to code some or all of them from scratch. The great thing is that Mule does not require you to learn an API to implement services. If you have existing POJOs and beans you can simply drop them in without modification. If you need to create them you simply focus on the function they are to perform.

This is because Mule uses an entry point resolver that passes the payload of a message to your service component, looking for a method that accepts an object of the same type as the payload (to learn more about Mule Messages see "Messages in Mule" later in this chapter). If it doesn't find such a method or finds more than one, it will throw an exception. There are ways to override this behavior: you can implement the `org.mule.api.lifecycle` Callable interface in your service component or use a different entry point resolver—one provided with Mule or one that you build yourself.

There is also a powerful API you can use when developing your service components. Using it gives you greater control over your component and full access to the Mule server hosting it; however, it also couples your components with Mule. Best practice dictates that you should keep your service components as loosely coupled as possible. We will explore some aspects of the API when we discuss unit testing in this chapter, and we will cover creating your own Mule components, such as routers and transformers, in Chapter 7.

Tip   You can learn more about creating service components at `http://mule.mulesource.org/display/MULE2USER/Developing+Service+Components`.

The Mule Configuration File

Once you have developed or copied the POJOs and beans that you will be using, you need to build your Mule configuration file and define how you want to wire your components together, specifying the routing, transports, and transformers to be used. We looked at how to create a Mule configuration in Chapter 1.

After you create your `config xml` file, ensure that it is located in the correct location—namely a folder that is in the `classpath` at the time Mule is launched. If this is not the case you will have to provide a fully-qualified path for the file when launching Mule.

The default name for this file is `mule-config.xml` but you can use any name for it. You can also split the file up into multiple files and include them as a comma-separated list, for example on the command line (see the next section, "Running Your Mule Application").

Running Your Mule Application

The simplest way to run Mule is to launch it from the command prompt, as this example shows:

```
"%MULE_HOME%\bin\mule.bat" -config bin/mule-config.xml
```

This will look for the Mule launch script in the `bin` folder of `MULE_HOME` (see the previous "Installing Mule" section) and will run Mule by loading the configuration file `mule-config.xml` from the `bin` folder located in the current folder.

The `-config` parameter allows you to specify a fully-qualified or relative path and file name for the configuration file to use as shown in the preceding code snippet. Assuming that you have the JDK installed on your computer and that it is configured properly, the single command listed previously will work from within a script. This will deploy the wrapper that will, in turn, launch Mule. This is the most common method used to deploy Mule as a stand-alone application.

If you have a single configuration file named `mule-config.xml` that is located in the folder from which you launch Mule, or is in the `classpath`, all you need to do is type `mule` at the command prompt This will launch Mule as a foreground process.

Mule can be launched programmatically by using the `org.mule.MuleServer` class. This class needs to be created and its constructor must accept a comma-separated list of configuration files that you want to use, as shown here:

```
MuleServer server = new MuleServer ("myConfig.xml,
    myOtherConfig.xml");
server.start (true);
```

Installing Mule as a Service (or Daemon)

Apart from being run in a stand-alone fashion, Mule can also be installed as a service on Windows or as a daemon on Unix.

On Windows use the `install` parameter shown here:

```
mule install -config myConfig.xml
```

This can be reversed by using the following `remove` command:

```
mule remove
```

Once installed, Mule can be started, stopped, or restarted. In each case the `config` parameter will accept a comma-separated list of configuration files to use:

```
mule start | restart | stop -config myConfig.xml
```

Additionally, you can use the following Windows `net` command to start and stop Mule:

```
net start | stop mule
```

On *nix you can use the `service` command to start, stop, and restart Mule, but this is only applicable if your OS supports SysV-style startup systems.

Tip   You can also deploy Mule by embedding it in a Java application, web application, application server, or Spring application. You can learn more about these options at `http://www.mulesource.org/display/MULE2USER/Deployment+Scenarios`.

To browse the Mule wiki for more information on running Mule, go to `http://www.mulesource.org/display/MULE2INTRO/Running+Mule`.

Unit Tests

Having a modeled application is not much help unless you can verify that the model functions the way it is supposed to. In this section we will investigate how you can test a Mule application, after which you will be able to implement such a test yourself.

Testing Applications

The simplest way to test an application—however large or small—is to repeatedly run the program, feed it various values, and ensure that the outputs are what they should be. Of course, in such a case, it is also simple to draw up a chart of which inputs should produce a particular series of outputs. Mule is no different, and while it can be launched from the command line, the rather lengthy log files can be particularly daunting to read, parse, and filter; especially if you're trying to debug a Mule application. The amount and type of entries in the log file can be adjusted by tweaking the logger settings, but this means that some useful information might be excluded, which can be counter productive.

An automatic series of tests would be the ideal solution since this will consistently run all the tests necessary to prove your application. The xUnit family of tests is the most commonly-used test framework. Pioneered in the 1990s by Kent Beck and Erich Gamma, the concept has been ported to numerous languages, including Java. In fact, the popularity of the Java language means that the JUnit family of tests is perhaps the most commonly used.

JUnit allows you to implement several testing paradigms. *Black box* testing involves testing the results of an application without knowing what the program's internals looks like. *White box* testing is the opposite, where the tests are intimately aware of how the program works. *Grey box* testing is a combination of both.

When testing a Mule application, we normally use black box testing.

The main advantage of a unit test is that it allows you to repetitively test the code using the same parameters. While developing, you can use the tests to see how successful your code is. These tests, if complete, can also serve as documentation for your classes—the more tests you have, the easier it is to see what the original application is meant to do.

Of course, such tests help make bug locating and fixing a lot easier since you only need to inspect the tests that fail to figure out where problems arise. It is good practice to always add new test cases with different scenarios and possibilities. This is useful when you need to refactor code at a later stage, or when you need to modify the original application or classes.

Black Box Testing a Mule Server

Figure 4-2 illustrates the communication between your test case and a Mule server. Test data is sent to the server in the form of data on one or more endpoints. These endpoints are read and the data processed according to Mule's configuration. The test case can then monitor the endpoints from which it is expecting results without knowing how the output is being generated.

Figure 4-2. Black box testing

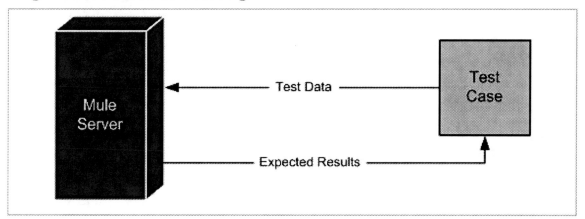

Black box testing involves being able to send information to an application and examine the output. The test will not contain any assumptions or details about the program itself; there is no way to tell, just by examining the test, how an input A causes an output B.

Mule applications can easily be tested in this manner since you can place information on a valid endpoint and, if your Mule server is properly configured, you will receive a result on another endpoint. You can compare this output with your expected results to make sure that your Mule server is properly configured.

Creating a Test Case

JUnit test cases are normally simple Java classes that can interact with the items that are under test. This is not enough for a Mule application since you need to make sure that a Mule server is loaded and available before it can be used. Mule has a Java class, `org.mule.tck.`
`FunctionalTestCase`, that can be used precisely for this sort of thing; this class can be found inside the `mule-tests-functional.jar`.

The `FunctionalTestCase` class takes care of all necessary Mule initialization and start-up processes and lets you focus on your test. All

JUnit tests that you want to write for Mule applications should extend FunctionalTestCase to avoid any unnecessary coding. The only variables that FunctionalTestCase needs are the location and name of the Mule configuration file. This can be achieved through a single method that has to be overridden—getConfigResources()—which is meant to return the full or relative path to the configuration file.

FunctionalTestCase will reinitialize the Mule server for every test that you create. This means that every test will cause Mule to be reloaded and connections to all external items, like JMS servers and databases, will be reconnected. This may be desirable in some cases but can also incur an overhead. This behavior can be changed by configuring FunctionalTestCase to reuse the same Mule instance. This is done by setting the DisposeManagerPerSuite flag to true.

The code in the following example shows an empty test suite that extends the FunctionalTestCase class and implements the getConfigResources() method. The relative path to the configuration file is relative to the Mule server's current directory.

```
package com.ricston.mule.training.examples;

import org.mule.tck.FunctionalTestCase;

public class testApplication extends FunctionalTestCase
{
    public void testFirstCondition() throws Exception{
      // TODO: Fill in code …
}

    protected String getConfigResources()
    {
        return "../conf/mule-config.xml";
    }
}
```

Before we can look at the integration test, we need to explain what a message means to Mule and what APIs there are to manipulate and control a Mule message.

Messages in Mule

Communication with a Mule server can be performed by placing a message on an endpoint. The endpoint can be any valid endpoint but what should the message look like?

Figure 4-3 shows all the different parts of a message in Mule.

Figure 4-3. The Mule message

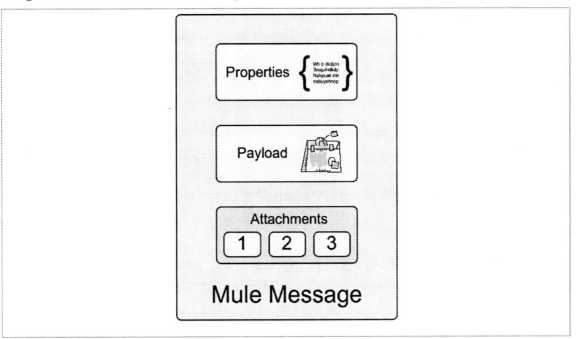

The MuleMessage Interface

Actual data received on an endpoint is packaged into an object that implements the MuleMessage interface. This object will contain the following:

- A series of properties that will vary depending on the transport in use.

- The entire data as the payload of the MuleMessage. This can be any sort of object.

- If applicable, a series of attachments that accompany the message.

Messages within a Mule instance are routed and handled as MuleMessage objects; however, it is the payload that is passed to the method that is to be executed. The same applies to the return value of a component; it is wrapped up as a payload of a MuleMessage. This layer of abstraction allows Mule elements such as routers and transformers to work with any data type independently of the communication protocols used.

Apart from the payload, a MuleMessage has a number of properties that contain metadata about the payload. These name-value pairs are heavily dependent on the transport used, for example; a JMS message will have a JMSPriority property that an SMTP message will not. The SMTP message, on the other hand, will have a From property.

All this conversion and encapsulation is totally transparent to the Mule developer since Mule handles the necessary conversions on demand. You will also need to create or manipulate MuleMessage objects if you need to send or receive messages programmatically, for example within unit tests.

MuleMessage Methods

A MuleMessage exposes the following methods, which allow you to inspect and manipulate the payload and the properties:

- getPayload() will retrieve the payload inside the MuleMessage. This will be the transformed payload.

- getPayload (Class) will retrieve the payload inside the MuleMessage and attempt to transform it to the specified class. Mule does this by using an internal registry of transformers that are available to best transform the payload into the required type.

- `getPayloadAsBytes()` will retrieve the payload inside the `MuleMessage` and convert it to a byte array.

- `getPayloadAsString()` will retrieve the payload inside the `MuleMessage` and convert it to a string.

- `getOriginalPayload()` will retrieve the untransformed payload.

- `setPayload(Object)` will override the current payload with the new object.

- `getProperty (String)` will return the value of a property as an object for a given name. If you know the data type of the property you can use specialized methods such as `getBooleanProperty()`, `getIntProperty()`, and so forth.

- `setProperty (String, Object)` will set the value of a property for a given name. If you know the data type of the property you can use specialized methods such as `setBooleanProperty` and `setIntProperty` rather than passing a generic object.

- `getPropertyNames()` will retrieve a map that contains all the names of all the properties.

- `getAttachment (String)` will retrieve a specific attachment. A `MuleMessage` can have multiple attachments.

- `getAttachmentNames()` will return a map containing a list of the names of all attachments.

- `addAttachment(String, DataHandler)` will add an attachment to the `MuleMessage`.

Tip   The JavaDocs contain a more complete description of this and all other Mule classes. They can be found on the MuleSource wiki at `http://www.mulesource.org`.

Implementing MuleMessage

There is one implementation of MuleMessage available in the org.mule package, called DefaultMuleMessage. This is nothing more than a wrapper object that contains the properties and payload of a message.

In code you can create MuleMessage or DefaultMuleMessage objects by constructing a new DefaultMuleMessage. Its constructor is overloaded to accept data that will be used as the payload. In the example that follows, the first line of code constructs a new variable called aMsg that will be a new DefaultMuleMessage object with a string payload. In the second example, the payload is initially empty:

```
MuleMessage aMsg = new DefaultMuleMessage("bc");
DefaultMuleMessage Msg = new DefaultMuleMessage();
```

Communicating with the Mule Server

One way of communicating with the Mule server is to use the MuleClient class. This class is available in the org.mule.module.client. MuleClient package and allows you to send and receive events to and from a Mule server. The following methods are available:

- dispatch(String, MuleMessage) will send a MuleMessage to the Mule server along a given endpoint asynchronously.

- send(String, MuleMessage,int) will send a MuleMessage to the Mule server along a given endpoint synchronously.

- sendAsync(String, MuleMessage) will send a synchronous MuleMessage to the Mule server without blocking, that is it will simulate asynchronicity.

- request(String,Long) will receive a message from the Mule server from the specified endpoint.

Asserting Output

You can verify a Mule server's output by comparing it with the expected result. JUnit provides you with a series of assertion statements that let you make these comparisons and that will raise exceptions if the assertion is not true. Your test case will therefore fail with the appropriate error message, clearly identifying which assertion has failed. The most common assertion statements are as follows:

- `assertNull()` checks that the object passed to it is a null object.

- `assertNotNull()` checks that the object passed to it is not null.

- `assertEquals()` checks that the two items passed to it are equal to one another. This method is overloaded to accept different data types.

- `assertTrue()` checks that the boolean condition passed to it evaluates to `true`.

- `assertFalse()` checks that the boolean condition passed to it evaluates to `false`.

- `assertSame()` checks that the two objects passed to it refer to the same object.

- `assertNotSame()` checks that the two objects passed to it do not refer to the same object.

Testing Mule Using JUnit

As an example, let's take a couple of simple Java objects—one that contains a single method that squares any integer it receives, and another that will inverse any integer it receives.

These two components will be hosted within a Mule server such that an integer passed along `vm://math` will be received by the first service. The result will be sent to the second class on `vm://inverse` and the result of this passed back along `vm://math`.

This is demonstrated in Figure 4-4. Note that since there is no outbound route defined for the inverse service, the result will be sent back along `vm://inverse` and then along `vm://math`. This will automatically be a synchronous process. Inside a test case we can send and receive along `vm://math`.

Figure 4-4. JUnit example

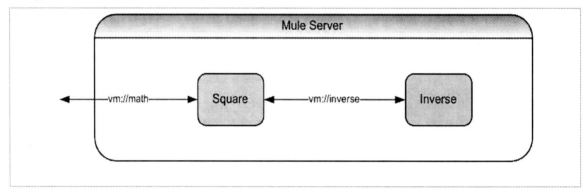

These are the Mule services for the example:

```
<service name="Square">
    <inbound>
        <vm:inbound-endpoint path="math"/>
    </inbound>
    <component class="com.ricston.tests.Square"/>
    <outbound>
        <outbound-pass-through-router>
            <vm:outbound-endpoint path="inverse"/>
        </outbound-pass-through-router>
    </outbound>
</service>

<service name="Inverse">
    <inbound>
        <vm:inbound-endpoint path="inverse" />
    </inbound>
    <component class="com.ricston.tests.Inverse"/>
</service>
```

Here we are not going to perform unit tests on the Square and Inverse POJOs—those would be done separately. The focus of the next test is to verify the Mule application—to check that the endpoints, routers, transformers, filters, and components *together* function as expected. This is commonly referred to as *integration testing*.

Next we have this source code for the test case:

```
public class testMuleMath extends
FunctionalTestCase {

public void testWithFive() throws Exception{
    MuleClient client = new MuleClient();
    MuleMessage reply = client.send
        ("vm://math", Integer (5));

        assertNotNull(reply);
        assertNotNull(reply.getPayload());
        Integer result = (Integer)reply.getPayload();
        assertEquals(result.intValue(),-25);
    }
}
```

There is only one test here—using the number 5 as an input, we're expecting the result to be -25. The lines of code with line numbers are explained in greater detail here:

- Construct a new `MuleClient` to be able to communicate with the Mule server.

- Send the number 5 to the endpoint called `vm://math` and wait for a reply. The reply will be saved into a new `MuleMessage` object.

- Assert that the reply is not null.

- Assert that the payload of the message is not null.

- Retrieve the payload and typecast it as an integer.

- Assert that this integer matches the expected result.

Note that this kind of test is a black box test—the test has no idea how the number 5 became the number -25; it merely confirms that it does. While we know that two POJOs were being used, if this is changed to include any number of POJOs, the test will still send and receive along vm://math and expect the result to be -25.

Tip   If you use global endpoints your XML config and test cases could reference endpoints by their logical name rather than physical representation, thereby reducing maintenance.

Summary

Modeling applications in Mule involves thinking about the different steps that need to be taken for individual services that Mule will host or interact with. Routers will govern how the data will flow from one service to another and transformers will be needed to convert data from one format to another.

The Mule application can be built from such a model by using VM channels initially to let you focus on the routing logic; you can replace these endpoints with the live transports once you are satisfied that the routing has been implemented properly.

As you build your Mule application you'll need to test and validate your model using JUnit and Mule's FunctionalTestCase class. Once you start creating tests, the MuleClient class lets you interact with a Mule server by sending messages (typically DefaultMuleMessage objects that implement the MuleMessage interface). Your tests can be confirmed using standard JUnit assertions.

Chapter 5: Mule Transports

In this chapter we are going to look at a few commonly-used transports and protocols that Mule supports. First, we're going to take a look at the overall architecture of a transport, what classes make up a transport, and how connectors are configured in general.

Transport Architecture

More than 26 transports are supported by Mule and available in the default installation. More are available through the developer community and there is a simple framework for you to develop your own.

Transport protocols are configured in Mule in a set of connector XML tags in the Mule configuration file. Every connector has a `name` attribute that lets you assign a unique name to each connector. All properties of a connector are defined here; while there are default values for most properties, some may need to be explicitly set before the connector can be used.

Endpoints also refer to the transport that is going to be used—generic endpoints refer to the transport in their address while transport-specific endpoints refer to the proper XML namespace. Most transport properties can be used and configured on an endpoint; in this case, properties on an endpoint will override the properties in the connector but only for the endpoint itself. Endpoints also have a `connector` attribute that will allow you to choose which connector to use for the endpoint. This is useful if you have multiple connectors as you would need to indicate which connector (and therefore group of settings) to use.

Connectors and Endpoints

A connector will know to create and use a message dispatcher, or message receiver class, once an inbound or outbound endpoint is going to be used.

The dispatcher and receiver classes will also use any relevant configuration on the connectors to be able to read or write data.

In the example that follows we have two instances of the STDIO transport with different configurations. An endpoint will have to indicate which STDIO connector it wants to use, as otherwise Mule will not know which group of settings to apply. This is done through the connector attribute of the generic or transport-specific endpoints.

```
<stdio:connector name="NameFromConsole"
    promptMessage="Type out a name"/>

<stdio:connector name="NumberToConsole"
    promptMessage="Your number is: "/>

<stdio:inbound-endpoint system="IN"
    connector="NameFromConsole"/>

<stdio:inbound-endpoint system="IN"
    connector="NumberToConsole"/>
```

A Transport

As Figure 5-1 shows, each transport in Mule is made up of the following items:

- A message receiver that knows how to handle an endpoint and read data from that endpoint.

- A message dispatcher that knows how to handle an endpoint and write data to that endpoint.

- Zero or more transport transformers.

Figure 5-1 – Transport Architecture

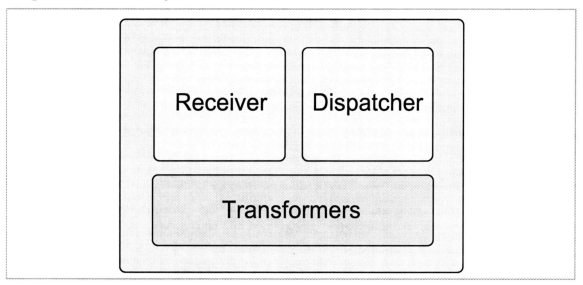

The MessageReceiver Interface

The MessageReceiver interface is implemented by objects that read data from an endpoint for a specific connector. The abstract implementation of this interface is `org.mule.transport.AbstractMessageReceiver`; polling receivers would inherit from `org.mule.transport.AbstractPollingMessageReceiver`. For transaction-aware receivers you should inherit from the `org.mule.transport.TransactedPollingMessageReceiver`.

The MessageDispatcher Interface

The MessageDispatcher interface is implemented by dispatcher objects that are contained and managed by the connector. These objects know how to send data along the underlying technology so they are unique to each transport. The abstract class—`AbstractMessageDispatcher`—provides support for handling threads and their lifecycles and validations so you won't have to do this yourself; apart from this the abstract class will execute the dispatch in its own thread if it is asynchronous.

Transport Overrides

While you can create new transports, more often than not all you may need to do is customize an existing transport for your own use. In fact, you may just want to change one class within the entire transport rather than create a completely new one.

Tip In most scenarios, just configuring the connection/endpoint will be sufficient to use a transport. However, in some scenarios it may be desirable to alter the existing behavior of the transport.

Each transport has a service descriptor file that is stored within the META-INF directory and is named according to the protocol that it represents. It is a standard Java properties file that contains a list of the internal classes used. You can change this file to indicate that you wish to use a different class, for example one of your own. Alternatively, service overrides can be more conveniently configured inside the XML file on the connector element.

Service Descriptor File

The main classes that can be changed are as follows:

- connector refers to the class that represents the entire connector. This class must implement the org.mule.api.transport.Connector interface.

- message.receiver refers to the MessageReceiver class to use.

- transacted.message.receiver and xa.transacted.message.receiver indicate which class to use for single-resource or XA transactions.

- The `inbound.transformer`, `outbound.transformer`, and `response.transformer` properties show you which transformers are applied by default if no transformations have been explicitly set on the endpoint.

Transports and Their Configuration

In the previous section, we spoke about how transports are configured and what classes are in use inside the transports, so now we can move on to the specifics of the commonly-used transports in a Mule application.

The Console Transport

The console transport provides a Mule application with access to the standard input and output devices, which typically would be the keyboard and monitor. This transport is mainly used in debugging and testing and is rarely used in production environments. The required XML namespace and schema are listed here and are also available from the MuleSource site:

```
xmlns:stdio=
  "http://www.mulesource.org/schema/mule/stdio/2.0"
xsi:schemaLocation=
"http://www.mulesource.org/schema/mule/stdio/2.0
  http://www.mulesource.org/schema/mule/stdio/2.0/
    mule-stdio.xsd"
```

Attributes

No connector is needed and default values for this transport's properties are usually sufficient. The following properties are available as attributes:

- `promptMessage` is an optional message that can prompt the user for input.

- `messageDelayTime` is the length of time to wait before prompting the user for input, in milliseconds. Defaults to 3000 (3 seconds).

- `outputMessage` is an optional message that is displayed before any output is displayed.

- resourceBundle refers to the name of the bundle to use if you are internationalizing your application.

- promptMessageCode is a numeric property that is a code number referring to a promptMessage to use from the resourceBundle.

- promptMessageCode is a numeric property that is a code number referring to a promptMessage to use from the resourceBundle.

- outputMessageCode is a numeric property that is a code number referring to an outputMessage to use from the resourceBundle.

Example

The following console connector is called SystemConnector and is configured to prompt users for input with a message of Please enter a flight code: after a delay of one second. Before displaying any output, the message The response is: is displayed.

```
<stdio:connector name="SystemConnector"
     promptMessage="Please enter a flight code: "
     messageDelayTime="1000"
     outputMessage="The response is: "/>

<stdio:inbound-endpoint system="IN"/>
<inbound-endpoint address="stdio://System.in"/>

<stdio:outbound-endpoint system="OUT"/>
<stdio:outbound-endpoint system="ERR"/>
```

The first two endpoints are inbound endpoints and are both the same; the first uses the transport-specific endpoint while the second is a generic endpoint. The second series of endpoints are both outbound endpoints and allow you to send output to the standard output device or to the standard error device. Normally, both of these refer to the monitor.

The Virtual Machine (VM) Transport

The VM transport is used for intra-VM communication between components managed by Mule. VM messaging can be both synchronous and asynchronous depending on how it is configured. It also supports transactions, which makes it the ideal transport to use for testing and simulating your Mule configuration. The required XML namespace and schema are listed here and are available from the MuleSource site:

```
xmlns:vm="http://www.mulesource.org/schema/mule/vm/2.0"
xsi:schemaLocation=
  "http://www.mulesource.org/schema/mule/vm/2.0
     http://www.mulesource.org/schema/mule/vm/2.0/
mule-vm.xsd"
```

Attributes

There is no host or configuration needed to set up a VM transport. The VM transport has only one attribute, queueEvents, which defaults to false.

```
<vm:connector name="myVM" queueEvents="true"/>

<vm:inbound-endpoint path="errorQueue"
    connector="myVM"/>
<inbound-endpoint address="vm://errorQueue"/>
```

This determines whether the messages will be transferred synchronously or asynchronously. If true, then queues will be created and the endpoint name will also be the name of the queue. If false, then the messages will be transmitted synchronously and delivered in a point-to-point fashion. The connector's queueEvents property cannot be configured on the endpoint; the VM transport needs to be constructed with the ability to either use queues internally or to deliver in a point-to-point fashion.

The preceding endpoint is therefore an asynchronous endpoint, since it is tied to the myVM connector.

Persistence

All VM queues can be configured to be persistent, which means that the items on the queues are persisted when the Mule server shuts down. All VM transports that are configured to be asynchronous can be configured to persist the items they contain. Check out this sample config:

```
<vm:connector name="myVM" queueEvents="true">
<queue-profile persistent="true"
      maxOutstandingMessages="1000"/>
</vm:connector>
```

The `queue-profile` child element for the VM transport allows you to specify whether you want to persist or not (the default is not to persist) and to indicate the maximum number of items that will be persisted. The default persistence strategy is to save the items on the VM queues to a file on disk.

Processing Queues

When a service is going to consume a message off a queue, the item at the front of the queue is removed and handled by the service. The queue will shrink and the second item in line will be in the front of the queue, as shown in Figure 5-2(a).

However, what happens when Mule is going to consume a message off a transport that does not use queues, such as the File transport for instance? In such a situation, the first file will be read and consumed but the file does not disappear from the underlying file system. If Mule tries to read from the same endpoint again, the same file will be re-read, as shown in Figure 5-2(b).

Figure 5-2 – Removing Messages from a Queue

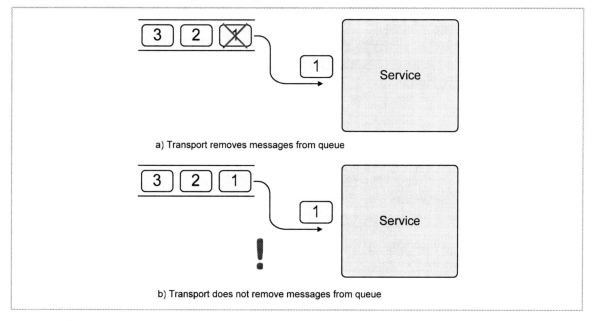

a) Transport removes messages from queue

b) Transport does not remove messages from queue

In such cases, the consumption of messages needs to be simulated. Let's take a look at how this is implemented in the File transport.

The File Transport

The File transport reads and writes files from and to the file system via network shares as well as mounted drives; as long as the directory is accessible to the operating system's file system, Mule will be able to consume or produce files.

This applies to both Windows and *nix file systems. The transport also has streaming support for large files. The required XML namespace and schema are listed here and are available from the MuleSource site:

```
xmlns:file=
  "http://www.mulesource.org/schema/mule/file/2.0"
xsi:schemaLocation=
  "http://www.mulesource.org/schema/mule/file/2.0
  http://www.mulesource.org/schema/mule/file/2.0/
    mule-file.xsd"
```

Attributes

The following is a list of commonly-used attributes for this transport:

- `pollingFrequency` is the frequency, in milliseconds, that the read directory should be checked. Note that the read directory is specified by the endpoint of the listening component.

- `fileAge` is a property that, if set, tells the connector to ignore files that have just been created unless they are a specified age old. This age is specified in milliseconds.

- `moveToDirectoryName` is the directory to which the file should be written once it has been read. This property helps simulate the consuming of a file. If this property is not set the file is deleted once read.

- `moveToPattern` is the pattern to use to build file names when moving a file that was read to a new location determined by the `moveToDirectory` property. This can use the patterns supported by the file name parser (see the next section) configured for this connector.

- `binary` indicates whether binary files are going to be read and written. Defaults to `false`.

- `streaming` indicates whether the file should be read in its entirety or streamed.

- `outputAppend` determines whether the file being written should append to an existing file, if one exists. Defaults to `false`.

- `outputPattern` is the pattern to use to build a file name when writing a file to disk. This can use the patterns supported by the `filenameParser` configured for this connector (see the next section).

- `writeToDirectory` is the directory to which the file should be written on dispatch. This path is usually set as an outbound endpoint; however, this allows you to explicitly force a single directory for the connector.

Parser Options

The default file name parser used by Mule is this `legacy-filename-parser`:

```
<file:legacy-filename-parser pattern=""/>
```

This parser understands the following patterns:

- `${DATE}` uses the full timestamp in the format of `dd-MM-yy_HH-mm-ss.SS`. This can be restricted or changed, for example, by using this format: `${DATE:yy-MM-dd}`.

- `${SYSTIME}` is the current system time, in milliseconds.

- `${UUID}` is an automatically-generated, universally-unique ID.

- `${ORIGINALNAME}` is the original file name if the file being written was read from another location.

- `${COUNT}` is an incremental sequential counter that is maintained on a per connector basis.

You can also use the following `expression-filename-parser` if you would rather use an expression language to create your patterns:

```
<file:expression-filename-parser pattern=""/>
```

XPath can be used, for instance, to extract XML properties from a file and use them within the file names. The following `custom-filename-parser` would be used if you have created a parser of your own and want to use that instead:

```
<file:custom-filename-parser>
```

Example

In this example you can see a file connector called `newOrders`, which will poll the inbound endpoints once every 600,000 milliseconds, or once every 10 minutes. After reading files, these are placed into a subdirectory called "processed," but renamed to have the system time inside their file names. When writing files out, the original file name will be used.

```
<file:connector name="newOrders"
                pollingFrequency="600000"
                moveToDirectory="./processed"
                moveToPattern="${SYSTIME}.xml"
                outputPattern="${ORIGINALNAME}"/>

<file:inbound-endpoint path="/temp/file"/>
<file:inbound-endpoint path="C:/temp/file"/>
<file:inbound-endpoint path="./temp/file"/>
<file:inbound-endpoint path="temp"/>
<file:inbound-endpoint path="//192.168.0.1/temp/"/>
```

All file endpoint addresses need to be valid file URIs. The first inbound endpoint listed here uses Unix-style path names starting with a forward slash; however, Windows-style URIs, such as the next three inbound endpoints, are all valid too. Windows network file resources can also be accessed using the URI shown in the last inbound endpoint in the preceding code example.

File Transport Transformers

The following two file transformers are bundled with the File transport:

- `FileToByteArray` will convert a file into a byte array:

  ```
  <file:file-to-byte-array-transformer>
  ```

- `FileToString` will convert a file into a byte array first and then convert it to a string using the current encoding:

  ```
  <file:file-to-string-transformer>
  ```

The HTTP Transport

The HTTP transport allows Mule messages to be sent and received over HTTP or HTTPS. Because it inherits from the TCP transport, properties from that connector can be used for HTTP too. The required XML namespace and schema are listed here and are available from the MuleSource site:

```
xmlns:http=
  "http://www.mulesource.org/schema/mule/http/2.0"
xsi:schemaLocation=
"http://www.mulesource.org/schema/mule/http/2.0
  http://www.mulesource. org/schema/mule/http/2.0/
    mule-http.xsd"
```

The XML namespace and schema for the HTTPS transport are identical to those in the previous code listing; simply substitute `https` for `http`, as shown here:

```
xmlns:https=
  "http://www.mulesource.org/schema/mule/https/2.0"
xsi:schemaLocation=
  "http://www.mulesource.org/schema/mule/https/2.0
    http://www.mulesource. org/schema/mule/https/2.0/
mule-https.xsd"
```

Properties

These are some of the commonly-used attributes for this transport:

- `proxyHostname`—if you need a proxy to access the Internet, then this attribute should contain the IP address or host name of the proxy server.

- `proxyPort`—if you need a proxy to access the Internet, then this attribute should contain the port number of the proxy server.

- `proxyUsername`—a username to use if the proxy requires authentication.

- `proxyPassword`—the password to use if the proxy requires authentication.

- `receiveBufferSize`—the buffer size used to read data; defaults to 64*1,024.

- `sendBufferSize`—the buffer size used to write data; defaults to 64*1,024.

HTTPS Transport Elements

The HTTPS transport does not add any further properties to those included in the HTTP transport, but it does have these additional child elements that are needed:

- `tls-client` refers to client key stores that contain certificates necessary for identification. It has a `path` attribute that indicates a relative or fully-qualified path to the store; a `storePassword` attribute is the password needed to unlock it.

- `tls-key-store` refers to key stores needed for the server. It has a `path` attribute that indicates a relative or fully-qualified path to the store. The `storePassword` attribute is the password needed to unlock it, and the `keyPassword` attribute is the password that unlocks the private key.

- `tls-server` refers to the key store that contains the public certificates of trusted servers. Its `path` attribute indicates a relative or fully-qualified path to the store and its `storePassword` attribute is the password needed to unlock it.

Example

Here's an example using an HTTPS connector called `partnerCommunication`:

```
<https:connector name="partnerCommunication">
    <https:tls-key-store path="bin/serverKeyStore"
         keyPassword="pr1vateKey"
         storePassword="passw0rd"/>

    <https:tls-client path="bin/clientStore"
         storePassword="cl1entPassword"/>
```

```
<https:tls-server path="bin/trustedServers"
        storePassword="trustPassw0rd"/>

</https:connector>
```

It uses three key stores:

- Its main key store is stored in a file called serverKeyStore under the bin directory, which can be unlocked using a password of passw0rd and whose private key is accessible using a password of pr1vateKey.

- Its client key store is in a file called clientStore in the same directory and can be accessed using the password cl1entPassword.

- Its collection of trusted server certificates is in a file called trustedServers in the same directory and can be accessed using a password of trustPassw0rd.

HTTP and HTTPS Endpoints

Following are some examples of HTTP and HTTPS endpoints:

```
<https:inbound-endpoint address="localhost:1234"/>
```

This first endpoint is an inbound HTTPS endpoint that will read from the localhost on port 1234.

```
<http:outbound-endpoint
        address="user:password@mycompany.com/x1"/>
```

This second endpoint, on the other hand, is an outbound HTTP endpoint that will send messages to http://mycompany.com/x1. This connection is meant to be secure; the credentials are encoded on the endpoint in the form of username:password and are set on the message using Basic-authentication encoding.

```
<inbound-endpoint address="http://localhost:8080/mine"
                  synchronous="true">
    <properties>
        <property name="Content-Type" value="text/html"/>
        <property name="Location"
                  value="http://mule.codehaus.org/"/>
        <property name="http.status" value="307"/>
    </properties>
</endpoint>
```

The last endpoint is a generic inbound endpoint that will read from port 8080. The properties set here are all properties for the `MuleMessage` itself.

HTTP Transport Transformers

The following four transformers are included with the HTTP transport:

- `<http-client-method-response-to-object-transformer>` transforms an HTTP client response to a `DefaultMuleMessage`.

- `<http-response-to-string-transformer>` transforms an HTTP client response to a string. All response headers are preserved.

- `<object-to-http-client-method-request>` transforms a `MuleMessage` into an `HTTPClient` `HTTPMethod` that represents an `HTTPRequest`.

- `<message-to-http-response>` transforms a `MuleMessage` into an HTTP response.

The FTP Transport

The FTP transport allows the transfer of files to and from a remote FTP server. Either a remote file will become available as a `MuleMessage`, or a `MuleMessage` will be converted into a file on an FTP server. The connector, configuration, and use of this protocol are similar to that of the File transport. Streaming is supported for transmission of large files.

The XML namespaces and schema required are listed and available from the MuleSource site:

```
xmlns:ftp=
    "http://www.mulesource.org/schema/mule/ftp/2.0"
xsi:schemaLocation=
  "http://www.mulesource.org/schema/mule/ftp/2.0
   http://www.mulesource.org/schema/mule/ftp/2.0/
      mule-ftp.xsd"
```

Attributes

Here are the most commonly-used attributes for this transport:

- `pollingFrequency` is the frequency with which to poll the FTP server for new files, in milliseconds. The directory to read will be defined as the endpoint, naturally. This property is required and defaults to 1,000 (1 second). This property can also be set on the endpoint.

- `binary` flags whether to use binary or ASCII file types for transfer; defaults to `true`. This can also be set on the endpoint.

- `passive` flags whether to use FTP passive mode to allow progress through firewalls; set to `true` by default. This can also be set on the endpoint.

- `filenameParser` is what controls how file name patterns are interpreted to create new file names. It defaults to the `legacy-filename-parser` that the File transport uses. All the patterns that can be used for the File transport can also be used here.

- `outputPattern` is the pattern to use to build a file name when writing a file to an FTP site. This can use the patterns supported by the `filenameParser` configured for this connector. This property is required and defaults to `${DATE}`. It can also be set as a property on an FTP endpoint.

- `validateConnections` validates FTP connections before use; while this will take care of a failed (or restarted) FTP server, there is the cost of an additional NOOP command packet being sent. It does increase overall availability, however.

Example

The following example shows an FTP connector called `newItems` that will poll any inbound FTP endpoint every 600 seconds (10 minutes) for binary files. It will use passive mode to pass through firewalls and will output files to FTP endpoints using the original file name, if available.

```
<ftp:connector name="newItems"
      pollingFrequency="600000"
      binary="true"
      passive="true"
      outputPattern="${ORIGINALNAME}"/>
```

The next example refers to an inbound FTP endpoint. The FTP server to connect to is `ftp.mycompany.com`, and this connection will be attempted using a username of `joe` and a password of `123456`. Once connected, the home directory will be used.

```
<ftp:inbound-endpoint address=
      "ftp://joe:123456@ftp.mycompany.com/~"/>
```

The SMTP Transport

The SMTP transport allows you to send mail through an SMTP server using the `javax.mail` API. A specific connector provides transport for SMTPS, which has several additional properties for security.

The required XML namespace and schema are listed here, and are available from the MuleSource site:

```
xmlns:smtp=
    "http://www.mulesource.org/schema/mule/smtp/2.0"
xsi:schemaLocation=
  "http://www.mulesource.org/schema/mule/smtp/2.0
   http://www.mulesource.org/schema/mule/smtp/2.0/
      mule-smtp.xsd"
```

Attributes

The following SMTP properties can be set on the URI of the endpoint or as properties of the endpoint, as well as within the connector. However, you can set up property values on the MuleMessage too; these will override any properties on the endpoint.

- authenticator is needed when sending authenticated SMTP requests. By default, Mule handles authentication by creating a default if there are user credentials set on the SMTP endpoint. Users can customize the authenticator by setting this property to point to their own authenticator. Authenticators must implement the javax.mail.Authenticator interface.

- bccAddresses is a comma-separated list of e-mail addresses to blind carbon copy to.

- ccAddresses is a comma-separated list of e-mail addresses to carbon copy to.

- contentType sets the default Mime content type for the outgoing messages.

- customHeaders is a map of custom properties that will be set on the outgoing message's header.

- fromAddress is the from address to set on the outgoing message. This attribute is mandatory.

- replyToAddresses is a comma-separated list of e-mail addresses that will receive replies to the e-mail.

- subject is (if set on the connector) a default subject for the outbound message if one is not set on the endpoint. By default this is an empty string.

SMTPS Transport—Attributes

Besides inheriting all the attributes from the SMTP connector, the SMTPS connector implements the following attributes too:

- socketFactory is the SSL socket factory to use; by default this is javax.net.ssl.SSLSocketFactory.

- `socketFactoryFallback` indicates whether to enable fallback; by default this is set to `false`.

- `trustStore` is the file location of a trust store.

- `trustStorePassword` is the password for the trust store specified.

While server credentials may be set on the endpoint, defaults can be set on the connector as usual.

Example

In this example, any e-mails sent using this connector will have a default subject of `Mule Server` and will automatically appear as having been sent from `someone@company.com`:

```
<smtp:connector name="EmailConnector"
      fromAddress="someone@company.com"
      hostname="smtp.company.com"
      subject="Mule Server"/>
```

In this next example, an e-mail to `anyone@company.com` will be sent through the `smtp.company.com` mail server. The username (`anyName`) and password (`123456`) to access the SMTP server are included as attributes.

```
<smtp:outbound-endpoint
      to="anyone@company.com"
      host="smtp.company.com" name="anyName"
      password="123456"/>
```

SMTP Transformers

Two common transformers allow you to convert plain e-mail messages into strings or vice versa. These transformers work with the body of the e-mail message.

- `<smtp:string-to-email-transformer>`—this transformer converts a string to a `javax.mail.Message`. It uses transformer attributes to determine the `to` field and does not handle attachments.

- `<smtp:email-to-string-transformer>`—you can convert a `javax.mail.Message` to a string using this transformer.

The JMS Transport

The Java Message Service (JMS) specification is a Sun standard for messaging middleware (sometimes called enterprise messaging). It allows for data and events to be exchanged between different applications by utilizing queues in a centrally-located server. This leads to the creation of message-based applications rather than autonomous silos. Messages sent to or received from a JMS server are done so asynchronously, which means that the server itself is loosely coupled to your application. Messages can also be transacted to preserve integrity.

A number of vendors supply JMS servers—WebLogicMQ, WebSphereMQ (previously MQSeries), and TIBCO EMS are the most common ones. Each vendor may implement one or both of the main versions of the standard— JMS 1.1 or JMS 1.0.2b.

Queues and Topics

Messages can be placed on one of two different data structures within a JMS server—queues or topics. A JMS queue, illustrated in Figure 5-3, is a standard message queue implemented within a JMS server. An application that places items on a JMS queue makes its messages available to other applications that can read this queue.

Figure 5-3. JMS Queues

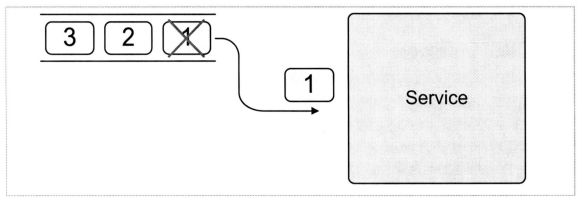

Topics (see Figure 5-4) differ from queues since they work on a publish/subscribe mechanism, which means any application that wants to read from the topic must subscribe to it first. You can have multiple subscribers on a single topic, with the result that when a new message is placed on the topic, all subscribers receive a single copy of it.

Figure 5-4. JMS Topics

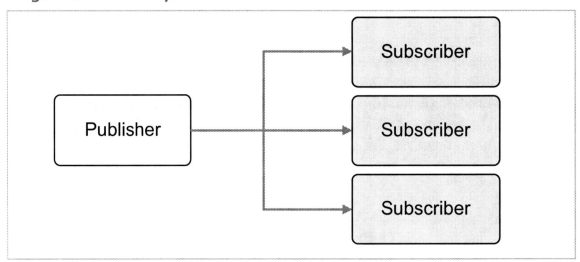

Depending on how the subscription is configured, a subscriber may or may not receive notification of items that were published when the subscriber was unavailable. The mechanism is very similar to RSS feeds, since multiple people can subscribe to the same feed and receive notification of new items on the feed even if they were unavailable at the time of publication.

The Transport

The Mule JMS transport can read and write to any JMS server that is 1.0.2b or 1.1 compliant. Although the JMS specification is a standard, different servers implement the specifications in different ways, so expect to find dedicated configurations in place. These settings may conflict, so a properly configured WebSphereMQ connector may not necessarily work with an ActiveMQ server. More information about server-specific settings is available on the MuleSource wiki.

Due to a restriction in the JMS API, you will need to configure separate Mule connectors to handle queues and topics if the server is JMS 1.0.2b–compliant; JMS 1.1 servers can use a single connector for either type of destination.

The required XML namespace and schema for the JMS transport are shown here, and are available from the MuleSource site:

```
xmlns:jms=
    "http://www.mulesource.org/schema/mule/jms/2.0"
xsi:schemaLocation=
  "http://www.mulesource.org/schema/mule/jms/2.0
   http://www.mulesource.org/schema/mule/jms/2.0/
      mule-jms.xsd"
```

Attributes

This list of attributes is not exhaustive; these are the most commonly-used ones. A complete list is available on the Mule wiki.

- `clientId` uniquely identifies the client and must be set if using durable subscriptions for topics. The JMS transport will set it for you automatically to `mule.<connector name>.<topic name>`, but some JMS servers expect you to set it directly. If the `clientID` is not unique, an `InvalidClientIDException` is thrown. This property is required if you use durable subscriptions.

- `durable` is used when a client wants to receive all messages posted on a topic, even ones that were published when the subscriber was inactive (a durable subscription). This can be overridden on an endpoint.

- `password` is used when connecting to a JMS server; this can be set on the endpoint.

- `specification` indicates whether this is a 1.0.2b or a 1.1 server; this property is required.

- `username` is the username to use when connecting to a JMS server; this can be set on the endpoint.

Tip   The connectors for specific JMS servers may have attributes of their own. For example, the ActiveMQ connector uses a `brokerURL` which is set to the URL that the JMS server is listening on.

Example

The following connector configuration defines a JMS connector to an ActiveMQ server; note the vendor-specific connector. This is a 1.1-compliant server, as you can see from the `specification` attribute, and its `brokerURL` is set to `vm://localhost`. In this case, connections to the JMS server will occur through Mule's JVM. The `durable` attribute is set to `true`, which tells us that this connector will be used for topics and that the subscriptions to all topics will be durable.

```
<jms:activemq-connector name="jmsConnector"
                        specification="1.1"
                        brokerURL="vm://localhost"
                        durable="true"/>
```

In this next set of examples, the first JMS inbound endpoint refers to a queue, while the second one refers to a topic. The queue and topic attributes are mutually exclusive as you can either refer to a queue or to a topic, but not both. The third endpoint is a generic inbound endpoint that shows how you can embed user credentials into the endpoint URI. Note that the topic in use is prefixed with the keyword topic:; queues do not need to be prefixed like this, but check the documentation for your JMS server.

```
<jms:inbound-endpoint queue="myQueue"/>
<jms:inbound-endpoint topic="myTopic"/>
<inbound-endpoint address=
                "jms://name:password@topic:myTopic"/>
```

This last endpoint example shows how you can use a JMS selector on a JMS endpoint. JMS selectors are JMS-specific endpoint filters. They differ from Mule filters in that you cannot use multiple selectors together.

```
<jms:inbound-endpoint queue="myQueue">
<jms:selector expression="JMSPriority=9"/>
</jms:inbound-endpoint/>
```

JMS Transformers

The JMS message-to-object transformer <jms:jmsmessage-to-object-transformer> converts javax.jms.Message objects, or subtypes, to generic Java objects. You can change the returnType attribute for this transformer to typecast the result further according to this list:

- javax.jms.TextMessage converts to a java.lang.String.

- javax.jms.ObjectMessage converts to a java.lang.Object.

- javax.jms.BytesMessage converts to a byte array. If the payload is compressed it will automatically uncompress it.

- javax.jms.MapMessage converts to a java.util.Map.

- `javax.jms.StreamMessage` converts to a `java.util.Vector` of objects from the Stream.

The object-to-JMS message transformer `<jms:object-to-jmsmessage-transformer>` does the opposite. Its `returntype` can be tweaked to typecast the JMS message too.

- `java.lang.String` converts to a `javax.jms.TextMessage`.

- `java.lang.Object` converts to a `javax.jms.ObjectMessage`.

- `byte[]` converts to a `javax.jms.BytesMessage`.

- `java.util.Map` converts to a `javax.jms.MapMessage`.

- `java.io.InputStream` converts to a `javax.jms.StreamMessage`.

Note   Mule Enterprise Edition includes a premium WebSphereMQ transport that supports specific configuration and behavior optimized for WMQ.

The JDBC Transport

The Java Database Connectivity (JDBC) transport connects to any relational database through the use of SQL statements. Inbound endpoints map to SQL SELECT statements to read data, and SQL INSERT statements are used to write data to a database, but UPDATE and DELETE statements can also be used. As with the File transport, queuing of messages needs to be simulated and so does consumption of messages. As we'll see this is achieved by using "acknowledge" queries.

The required XML namespace and schema for the JMS transport are shown here, and are available from the MuleSource site:

```
xmlns:jdbc=
    "http://www.mulesource.org/schema/mule/jdbc/2.0"
xsi:schemaLocation=
```

```
"http://www.mulesource.org/schema/mule/jdbc/2.0
 http://www.mulesource.org/schema/mule/jdbc/2.0/
    mule-jdbc.xsd"
```

Attributes

This list of attributes is not exhaustive; these are the most commonly-used ones.

- `dataSource-ref` is the name of the JDBC data source itself.

- `pollingFrequency` is the frequency with which to poll the database for new records, in milliseconds.

- `queryRunner-ref` is the name of the class used to execute queries. The default class used is `org.apache.commons.dbutils.QueryRunner`.

- `resultSetHandler-ref` is the name of the class used to pass query results back. The default class used is `org.apache.commons.dbutils.handlers.MapListHandler`.

The transport also has a child element where you can define the queries with the following syntax:

```
<jdbc:query key=" ... " value=" ... ">
```

Each query needs a key (which is a descriptive name for the query) as well as the actual SQL query itself. You can have multiple queries for a single JDBC connector. Three types of queries can be used:

- `read` queries are SELECT SQL statements that are bound to an inbound endpoint.

- `write` queries are usually INSERT SQL queries that are bound to an outbound endpoint.

- `ack` queries are executed immediately after a `read` query to mark the previously selected rows as having been processed. This type of query is identified with the same name as the `read` query, together with an .ack suffix. Typically these would be UPDATE SQL queries.

Example

The connector shown here is called `salesDB` and refers to a data source called `ordersDB` that is defined in Spring. It will poll for new records one time every second and will use the `salesOrderResultSetHandler` class to handle any rows returned by the respective queries.

```
<jdbc:connector name="salesDB"
    dataSource-ref="ordersDB"
    pollingFrequency="1000"
    resultSetHandler-ref="salesOrderResultSetHandler">

<spring:bean id="ordersDB"
    class="org.springframework.jdbc.datasource.
    DriverManagerDataSource">
    <spring:property name="driverClassName"
        value="com.mysql.jdbc.Driver"/>
    <spring:property name="url"
        value="jdbc:mysql://localhost:3306/orderdb"/>
    <spring:property name="username" value="myName"/>
    <spring:property name="password" value="myPwd"/>
</spring:bean>

  <jdbc:query key="getTest"
    value="SELECT ID, TYPE, DATA, ACK, RESULT FROM TEST
        WHERE TYPE =${type} AND ACK IS NULL"/>
  <jdbc:query key="getTest.ack"
    value="UPDATE TEST SET ACK = ${NOW}
        WHERE ID = ${id} AND TYPE =${type}
        AND DATA = ${data}"/>
  <jdbc:query key="writeTest"
   <jdbc:query key="writeTest"
      value="INSERT INTO TEST (ID, TYPE, DATA, ACK,
          RESULT)
      VALUES (NULL, ${type}, ${payload}, NULL, NULL)"/>

</jdbc:connector>
```

There are three queries set up here:

- The first query is an inbound query and will select the contents of five columns from the table called `test`, where the `type` field matches a parameterized value and the `ack` field is Null.

- The second query is an acknowledge query. It is characterized by having the same key but with an `.ack` suffix. Each row in the table that matches the criteria indicated will be updated so that the `ack` field will no longer be empty. This means that these rows will not be selected when the inbound query is re-run.

- The third query is an outbound query and will insert values into the correct columns in the table. The `${payload}` parameter refers to the payload of the current `MuleMessage`.

The following two endpoints are JDBC inbound and JDBC outbound endpoints, respectively, that refer to a specific query by name. In each case, we can configure any of the query parameters directly.

```
<jdbc:inbound-endpoint queryKey="getTest?type=1"/>
<jdbc:outbound-endpoint
    queryKey="jdbc://writeTest?type=1"/>
```

Note   Mule Enterprise Edition includes a premium JDBC transport that also supports stored procedures, cursors, and parameter parsing.

Summary

Transports are configured as connector elements in XML and are made up of a `MessageReceiver` class, a `MessageDispatcher` class, and zero or more transformers. The individual types of `MessageReceiver` classes differ depending on whether the transport is a polling- or listener-based transport. Having said that, the service descriptor file can always be inspected to see which classes are going to be used at runtime, and these settings can be overridden to change its behavior.

The first two transports we saw in this chapter—Console and VM—are invaluable for use in testing and debugging, and VM may also be used in production. While there is nothing to stop you using the Console transport in production, it has limited value. We also reviewed transports that implement standard Internet protocols such as HTTP, HTTPS, SMTP, SMTPS, and FTP transports.

We rounded out our tour of commonly-used Mule transports by taking a look at how Mule can tap into enterprise messaging mechanisms by using the JMS transport, and can read/write from/to a corporate database by using the JDBC transport.

This rounds out our discussion of the main transports in use in Mule. There are more transports available out of the box and on MuleForge. The manner in which they are configured is similar. It is worth visiting the information on the MuleSource wiki to figure out how to work with them.

Chapter 6: Web Services in Mule

Another set of transports in use in Mule are those related to web services. First we're going to see how Mule can host or connect to web services using the new CXF transport. Mule still also includes support for Axis, but the default transport for web services is CXF; it replaces the XFire transport, which in Mule 2.0 has been moved to MuleForge.

We do recommend using CXF for web services unless your project requires that you use the RPC/Encoded method. If this is the case then Apache Axis is the way to go. We'll examine the features inside this transport in the second part of this chapter.

Overview

Web services are nothing more than services that are available over a network—be it an internal network or the Internet—that adhere to the Simple Object Access Protocol (SOAP) and Web Services Descriptive Language (WSDL) protocols. A client application that wants to make use of these services can invoke them by using XML messages that are crafted on the SOAP standard. Such a request is understandable to a web service and it will return a response back to the client. If a client does not know what operations a web service provides, the WSDL for the service can be queried to see what operations are supported before the request is made.

Web services can be created using any technology—Axis, CXF, and .NET being the most popular—and clients can invoke web services using any technology too. Mule allows us to use web services by providing an Axis and a CXF transport.

Simple Object Access Protocol

The Simple Object Access Protocol (SOAP) defines the three parts described here to every message:

- An **envelope** describes what is in the message and how it can be processed. Each SOAP message is an envelope together with one body and zero or more headers.

- The **encoding rules** define a serialization mechanism to allow application-defined data types to be exchanged between different applications. Normal SOAP encoding is not supported by international standards, so interoperable web services are encouraged to avoid using any encoding. This is referred to as "literal encoding."

- The **communication style** is either RPC or message oriented. RPC is typically used with SOAP, while "document" style requires more programming work but offers a lower layer of abstraction.

Mule and Web Services

Figure 6-1 shows how Mule can interact with web services. On the left side of the diagram we can see that a third-party item (such as an application) is making a web service call, which refers to a service that is hosted in Mule. This web service call is nothing more than an inbound endpoint for the service. By using inbound web service endpoints Mule can host web services that are accessible to any other application.

On the right side of the diagram we can see that a service in Mule is making a web service call to a third-party item. This web service call is nothing more than an outbound endpoint for the service. By using outbound web service endpoints, Mule can connect to web services hosted by any other application.

In Mule you can configure a component to have a web service as an inbound endpoint. This will cause the component to be hosted as a web service; it will be visible to outside applications as a web service automatically. When a request is received, your component will be invoked.

A component can also be configured to have a web service as an outbound endpoint. This will cause Mule to transform the original request into a

SOAP request and route it to a web service. The web service can be hosted either locally or remotely.

Figure 6-1. Mule and Web Services

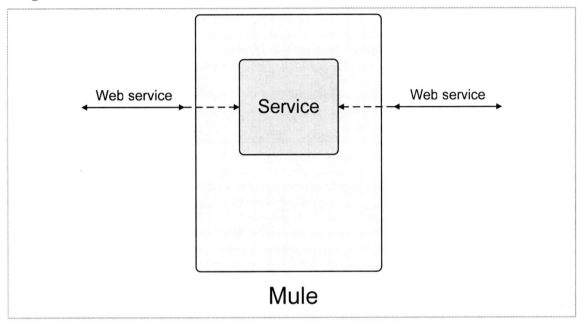

The web service may also be hosted inside a Mule instance or it could be an external web service. External web services can be constructed using any technology that implements the web services standards, for example Axis, XFire, or .NET. These all require different configurations as we shall see.

Data is transferred through an XML packet across the HTTP transport, which is implicitly used when you define web service endpoints. SOAP can also be used across other transports such as JMS.

The CXF Transport

Apart from Axis, Mule provides the CXF transport for SOAP support. In previous versions of Mule this was called the XFire transport and was implemented as the XFire engine. After looking at the evolution of the XFire transport to CXF, we will see how this protocol can be used inside a Mule application.

From XFire to CXF

XFire is a Java SOAP framework that provides an easy-to-use API to build web services. It uses a low-memory model based on STaX (Streaming API for XML) that delivers high performance and can be used over HTTP, JMS, XMPP, and VM transports. An XFire transport is included with Mule 1, but as mentioned previously, for Mule 2 it has been moved to MuleForge.

In 2006, the Celtix and XFire communities merged to provide a single web service platform, CXF (the name is based on the merging of Celtix and XFire). The result is an Apache project that provides an easy-to-use API that lets you build services that can communicate using SOAP, RESTful HTTP, or CORBA over HTTP, JMS, VM, or JBI.

The CXF Connector

CXF uses the Java API for XML Web Services (JAX-WS) standard, which is a series of APIs and annotations that allow you to easily build web services. In Mule it normally operates over HTTP, but it can be used across the other transports too.

The required XML namespace and schema are listed here, and are available from the MuleSource site:

```
xmlns:cxf=
  "http://www.mulesource.org/schema/mule/cxf/2.0"
xsi:schemaLocation=
  "http://www.mulesource.org/schema/mule/cxf/2.0
   http://www.mulesource.org/schema/mule/cxf/2.0/
     mule-cxf.xsd"
```

Attributes

One key attribute on the CXF connector is the `defaultFrontend` attribute, which allows you to specify that your CXF web services do not contain any JAX-WS annotations. By default this is set to `jaxws`, but you can change it to `simple` if your classes do not have annotations.

The endpoint attributes are as follows:

- `frontEnd` is the endpoint-level attribute for the `defaultFrontend` attribute.

- `wsdlLocation` lets you specify a location for the WSDL file if you do not want the CXF transport to create one automatically for you.

None of these attributes are required.

Hosting a CXF Web Service

Services in Mule can become CXF web services provided they have an inbound CXF endpoint. The most significant consideration is whether you can, or want to, use annotations.

Simple Front-End Implementation

If your classes are POJOs that cannot use annotations, you will need to implement your web service via your Mule configuration. This approach means you do not need to modify any code and makes it the ideal approach for migration from XFire and previous Mule versions. The web service would be configuration-driven since every setting will be included in the Mule configuration file.

Here's an example of a simple front end to any CXF web service implemented in Mule:

```
<cxf:connector name="CXFConnector"
               defaultFrontend="simple"/>
```

The preceding code snippet shows how the CXF connector can be configured to use the `defaultFrontend` attribute so that it will not look for the annotations within the hosted classes. Setting this attribute here will enable it for all endpoints, but you can configure this on an endpoint-by-endpoint basis using the endpoint's `frontend` attribute as shown in the following example:

```
<service name="ticketStatus">
    <inbound>
        <cxf:inbound-endpoint frontend="simple"
            address="http://10.0.0.1/status"/>
    </inbound>
    <component class="com.ricstonairways.Ticket"/>
</service>
```

Caution   A port should always be set. If you do not specify one, a default value of -1 will used.

Using Annotations

You can also use JAX-WS annotations in your classes to describe the CXF web service. You will need to create an interface to the class that you wish to host as a web service and annotate this class according to the JAX-WS API. You can also include references to an existing WSDL if you develop by contract rather than let the CXF transport generate the WSDL for you.

A key benefit of annotations is that they provide you with a short and concise manner in which to describe your web service. This "shorthand" reduces the amount of code that is needed.

Our next example shows an interface to a class that we will then use as a web service. It has a single method that returns the status for an airline ticket represented by the passenger name record (PNR) identifier.

```
package com.ricstonairways;

import javax.jws.WebService;

@WebService

public interface StatusInterface
    { String getStatus(String paxRecord); }
```

Note   We are importing the JAX package and annotating the interface by using the @ notation to indicate that this interface will be used as a web service.

The class that implements the previous interface is shown in the next example. It is annotated to show which interface is going to be used and the name of the web service.

```
package com.ricstonairways;

import javax.jws.WebService;

@WebService(endpointInterface ="com.ricstonairways.
StatusInterface", serviceName = "PNRStatus")

public class statusRetrieval implements StatusInterface
{
    public String getStatus (String paxRecord) {
        return paxList.find (paxRecord).status;
    }
}
```

The Mule configuration shown here allows us to host this annotated class as a CXF web service. It is similar to the configuration shown earlier but without the frontEnd attribute.

```
<model name="CxfExample">
    <service name="ticketStatus">
        <inbound>
            <cxf:inbound-endpoint address=
                "http://10.0.0.1/status"/>
        </inbound>
        <component class="com.ricstonairways.
                statusRetrieval"/>
    </service>
</model>
```

You can invoke this web service from within a web browser by using the
`http://host/service/OPERATION/PARAM_NAME/PARAM_VALUE` format,
which would look like this URL: `http://10.0.0.1/status/`
`ticketStatus/flightStatus/flightCode/RA1234`.

Programming by Contract

If the WSDL is defined before you start creating classes and services, then
this is known as contract-first programming. In such cases, you would not
want the CXF transport to generate a WSDL automatically but use an
existing one. You also need to be sure that the classes in use match the
descriptions in the WSDL file.

Tip   We recommend that you adopt this model as your preferred
approach; most people developing web services are moving to contract-first
programming.

Using a WSDL-to-Java tool, you can create an interface based on the
existing WSDL file and implement this interface in your class. Such a class
can then be used in the same way we've just seen.

Alternatively, the external WSDL file can be referred to from within the
JAX `@WebService` annotation or on a Mule endpoint directly. References

can be made to a WSDL file that is located on the classpath, somewhere on the file system, or to a resource somewhere in a web application.

```
@WebService(endpointInterface =
    "com.ricstonairways.StatusInterface",
    serviceName = "PNRStatus",
    wsdlLocation="./Status.WSDL")
```

In the preceding example, the location of the WSDL file is defined within the @WebService annotation inside the Java class. The next example shows how you can achieve the same effect by referring to the WSDL file from the inbound endpoint of your Mule configuration:

```
<cxf:inbound-endpoint
    address="http://10.0.0.1/status"
    wsdlLocation="./Status.WSDL"/>
```

This can be a valid reference to the file system, a file on the classpath, or a resource within your web application.

CXF Outbound Endpoint

The CXF transport allows you to use a CXF-generated client as an outbound endpoint. This client needs to be generated using the WSDL-to-Java tool mentioned earlier. The foreign web service can be local (on the same machine) or remote, and can be built using any web technology. As long as a valid WSDL is available, the CXF outbound endpoint can be used.

These are the attributes to configure on the endpoint:

- clientClass is a reference to the class that was generated with the WSDL-to-Java tool.

- wsdlPort is a reference to the WSDL port that you want to use to talk to the service.

- wsdlLocation is a reference to the WSDL file.

- `operation` is the name of the operation to invoke on the web service. The objects passed to the endpoint must match the signature of the method for this operation. If the operation takes in multiple parameters, they must be put in an `Object[]` array.

In the following example the CXF outbound endpoint has a valid address as before, which refers to the web service to invoke. The `clientClass` attribute refers to the class generated by the WSDL-to-Java tool for the WSDL file specified in the `wsdlLocation` attribute. The operation to invoke on this web service is the `getTicket` method.

```
<outbound>
    <outbound-pass-through-router>
        <cxf:outbound-endpoint address=
            "http://www.ricstonairways.com/buyTicket"
            clientClass="com.travelagent.buyTicket"
            wsdlLocation=""http://www.ricstonairways.com/
                wsdl/MA_BuyTicket.wsdl"
            operation="getTicket"/>
    </outbound-pass-through-router>
</outbound></service>
```

The Axis Transport

The Axis transport publishes components as Axis web services, or connects to web services using the Axis engine. In either case Mule uses an HTTP connector with default values and routes messages over HTTP to or from web services. However, SOAP messages can be transmitted over the JMS and VM transports using Axis. E-mail should also be supported but is not working properly at the time of writing.

Axis web services use the RPC/Encoded style by default. You can change this at an endpoint level so that web service invocation will use the correct style, but (on the inbound side) Mule-hosted services cannot be exposed as "Document/Literal" using the Axis connector. The required XML namespace and schema are listed here, and are available from the MuleSource site:

```
xmlns:axis=
  "http://www.mulesource.org/schema/mule/axis/2.0"
xsi:schemaLocation=
  "http://www.mulesource.org/schema/mule/axis/2.0
   http://www.mulesource.org/schema/mule/axis/2.0/
     mule-axis.xsd"
```

Axis Connector Attributes

This list of attributes is not exhaustive but these are the most commonly used ones:

- `clientConfig` refers to the configuration file to use when building an Axis client. This is used for Axis outbound endpoints only.

- `serverConfig` refers to the configuration file to use when building an Axis server. This is used for Axis inbound endpoints only.

- `treatMapAsNamedParams` controls how maps are interpreted by the connector. By default, the Axis connector assumes that a map contains multiple named parameters and unpacks them accordingly. If, however, your service expects a map, this will cause problems, so you will need to set this parameter to `false`.

The Axis connector has the following child element:

- While Axis can handle the serialization of primitive data types on its own, it would not know how to handle complex data types. Any nested data types need to be declared within the `bean-type` element. For example; if you had an object called `org.mule.student` that has an attribute of type `org.mule.person.address`, you will need to add `org.mule.person.address` to this list. You can define multiple `bean-type` elements for a single Axis connector.

Unlike other transports, Axis allows you to set up properties on the endpoints that are not configurable at a connector level.

- `wsdlFile` lets you define a WSDL file to use for an inbound endpoint. This makes sense if you want to use an existing WSDL file (for example, if you are developing by contract), as otherwise you could let Axis generate the WSDL automatically for you.

- `style` refers to the SOAP style to use and can be set to RPC, DOCUMENT, MESSAGE, or WRAPPED.

- `use` refers to the manner in which the SOAP packet will be used and can be set to ENCODED or LITERAL.

Axis endpoints also have child elements that refer to the options for this web service call.

- The Axis `options` element lets you include a comma-separated list of `allowedMethods` to expose. By default this is set to *, meaning "all."

- You can also configure the `bean-type` classes as elements on endpoints instead of on the connector.

- The `soap-service` child element lets you specify an `interface` that a Mule-hosted component implements. By listing the interfaces you want to expose, you can restrict which methods can be invoked on this component. It is similar to using the `axis:options` but here you have the option to specify an interface rather than list methods one by one.

Hosting an Axis Web Service

Here we have a simple Mule service that hosts the `com.ricstonairways.environment.weatherService` component. It has a single inbound web service endpoint that exposes the component as a web service on `http://localhost:81/WeatherService`.

```
<service name="WeatherService">
   <inbound>
      <inbound-endpoint address=
            "axis:http://localhost:81"/>
   </inbound>
   <component class="com.ricstonairways.environment.
                        weatherService"/>
</service>
```

Note   The WeatherService component must implement an interface. The methods in this interface will be available for clients of this web service.

Clients can then retrieve the WSDL for the web service or invoke any of the methods within this class by adding ?WSDL to the URL as a parameter, as shown here:

```
http://localhost:81/WeatherService?WSDL
```

The required parameters can also be encoded on the URL, for example to specify the method to invoke and the location for which weather data is required.

```
http://localhost:81/WeatherService?method=getWeather&
   town=London
```

Connecting to an Axis Web Service

Mule applications can invoke Axis web services by using a web service outbound endpoint as shown here:

```
<service name="WeatherService">
   <inbound>
      <inbound-endpoint address="vm://fromClient"/>
   </inbound>
   <bridge-component/>
   <outbound>
      <outbound-pass-through-router>
         <outbound-endpoint address=
             "axis:http://10.0.0.1:81/
               weatherService?method=getWeather"/>
      </outbound-pass-through-router>
   </outbound>
</service>
```

Caution   The `outbound-endpoint` `address` is split over two lines and should be joined into one contiguous URL in a working configuration.

Here, a bridge component is used to forward the message received on the VM `fromClient` queue to the web service. While the endpoint needs to have the method name included on it, the `MuleMessage` payload will be used as the parameter for the web service.

In this case the web service may exist locally, that is on the same computer, or on another machine. You will only need to change the IP address or computer name.

Invoking Non-Axis Web Services

If you want to invoke a web service that is not an Axis web service, you will need to adjust the outbound endpoint to handle this. The Axis transport cannot automatically handle non-Axis web services, so most of the properties need to be configured manually. You can get the information about the foreign web service by looking at the WSDL for it.

You then need to configure the following:

- The SOAP action format. This can be done automatically by Mule but needs to be explicitly configured if invoking .NET web services.

- The namespace. Declare the full name of the method being invoked (including the URL).

- The parameters used. This is a list of the names and types of all parameters that the method accepts. Some web services expect you to name the parameters and will raise exceptions if you try and invoke them without naming them first.

- The return type of the method. Similar to the previous point, the return type of the method may also need to be defined.

This example demonstrates how to invoke a non-Axis web service by using an outbound router collection with a single outbound router that will pass the Mule message to an Axis endpoint:

```
<outbound>
    <outbound-pass-through-router>
        <axis:outbound-endpoint address=
            "axis:http://10.0.0.1:82/weatherService?
            method=getWeather"
            soapAction="http://localhost:82/${method}">
                <axis:soap-method method="getWeather">
                    <axis:soap-parameter
                        parameter="city"
                        type="string"
                        mode="IN"/>
                    <axis:soap-return type="string"/>
                </axis:soap-method>
        </axis:outbound-endpoint>
    </outbound-pass-through-router>
</outbound>
```

Note   The axis:outbound-endpoint address is split over two lines and should be joined into one contiguous URL in a working configuration.

Because the web service being invoked is not an Axis web service we need to configure the following items:

- The `soapAction` attribute for the outbound endpoint. This indicates which method is going to be invoked and can be retrieved from the WSDL. The parameterized value in this example refers to the `method` encoded in the endpoint address.

- The `soap-method` child element for the outbound endpoint. This element describes the method that is going to be invoked. Its `name` attribute refers to the name of the method and should match the method listed in the `soapAction` attribute.

- The `soap-parameter` child elements for the `soap-method` element. Each of the method's parameters needs to be listed here. The `parameter` attribute is the name of the parameter, the `type` refers to the data type, and the `mode` refers to whether this parameter is going to be changed by the web service and sent back. Valid values for this attribute are `IN`, `OUT`, or `INOUT`. In our example we have a single string parameter called `city` that is set to `IN`. You can have multiple `soap-parameter` elements.

- The `soap-return` child element for the `soap-method` element. This describes the return value of the web service. Its attribute, `type`, lets you specify what data type the return value is.

REST

Representational State Transfer, otherwise knows as REST, is receiving a lot of attention as a better way of implementing web services. REST is actually the software architecture on which the world wide web is built and is not really anything new. It offers a simple yet powerful way of exposing and accessing web services that use an interface (HTTP+XML) with which most developers are already familiar, doing away with the need to learn about the SOAP specification and the accompanying baggage (for example tools) typically required to implement it.

Since Mule includes an HTTP transport and support for XML, you could therefore say that it inherently supports REST; however, the MuleSource team has gone one step further and added the Mule RESTpack to provide you with everything you will need to build RESTful applications with Mule.

Since these are not part of the core distribution, and to really do REST justice, we'd need to write an entire chapter on the subject; we cannot cover it in any detail here in this edition of our book. That will come later in the follow-up edition—please be patient! In the meantime you can learn more and download the RESTpack by pointing your browser at the Mule wiki at `http://mule.mulesource.org/display/MULE/Mule+RESTpack`.

Summary

This chapter focused on how Mule can connect to or host web services using endpoints that match a SOAP protocol. Mule does this using two specific transports—Axis and CXF. CXF is an extension to the XFire transport and is based on the JAX-WS API.

We can make use of the CXF transport to host a web service by using the default front end (mainly for compatibility reasons) or by creating dedicated interfaces and classes that are annotated with JAX-WS API annotations. You can also combine these two approaches with an existing WSDL file if necessary.

Connecting to a web service using the CXF transport is a matter of configuring the outbound endpoint to refer to a class that is generated for you based upon the WSDL file of the foreign web service.

Finally we added a brief reference to REST, the alternative, and many would argue superior, method to implementing and exposing web services building on the core protocols that power the world wide web and make it so scalable and resilient.

Chapter 7: Extending Mule

Building Mule elements is a fundamental task when putting Mule applications together. The first section in this chapter covers the abstract and base classes and interfaces to use to build your own Mule transformer. In the sections that follow we will examine how you can create a Mule filter and a Mule router.

Building a Transformer

A transformer in Mule is nothing more complex than a simple Java class that converts data from one type of object (or structure) to another. It is meant to facilitate the conversion from one sort of object (or structure) to another, and will work on in-flight data before the service component receives the Mule message or after the component has dispatched a Mule message, depending on the direction of the message (inbound or outbound respectively).

Some transformers are available out of the box; these are typically transport-specific transformers such as `JMSMessageToObject`. On the other hand, transformations that work on the data in your application are highly specialized and aren't normally available inside Mule.

You can implement a new transformer by implementing the Mule Transformer interface inside your class, but there is a fair amount of code that you'd need to re-do, so using the `AbstractTransformer` class would be the more practical route to take in most cases. This class implements a number of common methods and implements the Transformer interface so all you need to do is implement one single method to get your transformer up and running.

Transforms: ESB or Service?

The Enterprise Service Bus (ESB) industry is awash with opinions about transformations, but two schools of thought are prominent:

- Transformation occurs within the bus. This is what Mule does and is the recommended approach, as it allows you to code reusable transformers that are distinct from the business logic.

- Transformation should be nothing more than a service in its own right. While this is overkill, you can achieve some performance improvement in Mule if you have a processor-intensive transformation. You can also let an external item plugged into the bus perform any transformations it needs to.

Mule is flexible enough to allow you to use either approach, depending on which makes the most sense to you and does not impose any design choice on you. We are going to focus on the first, traditional approach in this section.

Introducing AbstractTransformer

`AbstractTransformer` is the class to use when building your own transformer. You can use the Transformer interface of course, but you will need to implement some, if not all, of the methods in the interface, so the class is a better starting place in most cases. Let's run through an example before looking at the methods and properties of this class.

Taking an airline seat booking as an example, the process to successfully book a seat results in a confirmation of the booking distributed via e-mail to the customer.

In Mule we could configure an outbound router collection to use a multicasting router to send the message to a database (say along a JDBC endpoint) and to the customer (along an SMTP endpoint). For this latter route we would need a transformer that converts a `bookedSeat` class into an e-mail.

The transformer will need to create the body of the e-mail using details from the message itself. All transformation will occur within the `doTransform()` method if we inherit from the `AbstractTransformer` class as follows:

```
protected Object doTransform(Object src,
    String encoding) throws TransformerException
{
    Booking aBooking = (Booking) src;

    return "Dear "+aBooking.passengerName
        +"We would like to inform you that "
        +"your seat on Flight"
        +aBooking.FlightNumber+" leaving "v
        +aBooking.OriginAirport+" on "
        +aBooking.DepartureDate+" at "
        +aBooking.DepartureTime+" is confirmed."
        +"  Please print out this e-mail and "
        +" present it to the check-in desk when"
        +" you arrive at the airport. Reference"
        +" number: "+aBooking.PNR";
}
```

In this code sample we have the transformation logic for the `BookingToConfirmation` transformer. The first thing to do is confirm that the object received really is what we're expecting, and then we can craft the full e-mail body by using the fields inside the `Booking` class received.

Mule allows transformers to register which classes they can handle. This is done in the constructor—essentially a transformer will tell Mule on initialization which items it can transform. In our case, the transformer can handle `Booking` classes, so our constructor looks like this:

```
public BookingToConfirmation()
{
    registerSourceType(Booking.class);
}
```

A transformer may be able to handle multiple source types, in which case, multiple items may be registered in the constructor.

Next we need to configure our transformer on the outbound endpoint.

```
<custom-transformer name="BookingToEmail"
    class="com.ricstonairways.ticketing.transformers
         .BookingToConfirmation"/>

<service name="PaymentService">
    <inbound>
        <vm:inbound-endpoint address="confirmedBookings"/>
    </inbound>
    <component class="com.ricstonairways.payment"/>
    <outbound>
        <outbound-pass-through-router>
            <smtp:outbound-endpoint to="customer@isp.com"
                    transformer-refs="BookingToEmail"/>
        </outbound-pass-through-router>
    </outbound>
</service>
```

At the beginning of this example, a custom transformer is declared and refers to the BookingToConfirmation class that we created previously. It is named BookingToEmail, and this name is then used on endpoints.

The service shown reads messages off a VM queue and returns its results to an e-mail address. This e-mail will contain the details of the booking as the e-mail body.

To round out our description of the AbstractTransformer class we will list the methods and properties it contains. Here are the methods:

- checkReturnClass is a protected method that confirms the object matches the value of the returnClass property, if set.

- doTransform is an abstract method that must be implemented in classes that inherit from this class. It should contain the actual transformation logic.

- `generateTransformerName` is used to automatically generate a name if it is needed but is not set.

- `isAcceptNull` is a public method that returns `false`. It can be overridden to let a transformer accept null values.

- `isSourceTypeSupported` checks the list of `sourceTypes` to validate whether a specific class type is supposed to be supported by the transformer.

- `registerSourceTypes` lets you add a source type to the list of accepted source types. This can be reversed using the `unregisterSourceType` method.

The class has the following properties:

- `endpoint` refers to the endpoint that this transformer is configured on.

- `ignoreBadInput` lets the transformer ignore any input that is not supported.

- `logger` refers to the Log4J class to use.

- `name` is a unique name that can be configured or automatically generated by the `generateTransformerName` method.

- `returnClass` lets a transformer be configured to return a specific type.

- `sourceTypes` is a list that contains all the source types the transformer can handle.

Building a Filter

After transformations, the second most common Mule element to be extended or coded is the filter. Filtering is a very common pattern, but the available filters may not be sufficient for application-specific needs. This section shows how a filter needs to be designed and built and then used within Mule.

Overview

Filtering is the ability to choose which messages to route, whether within an inbound or outbound message flow. The inbound router required for filtering is the `SelectiveConsumer` router, while the `FilteringOutboundRouter` is its outbound counterpart. A number of the other inbound and outbound routers in Mule inherit from these two respectively; also many routers in Mule implement commonly-used filtering patterns.

Each filter is expected to return a boolean value that indicates whether the message should be accepted or not. The router does not need to know any further specifics and will operate according to the boolean value that the filter returns. The filter needs to check a specific expression against the current message, which typically would be encoded as a property inside the configuration file. This expression can operate on a Mule message, that is, it can look at any value in the payload or the properties of the `MuleMessage`.

The Filter interface has a single method, `accept()`, that needs to be implemented. This method accepts a single, non-null `MuleMessage` and should return a boolean value that indicates whether this message passes the filter or not. The `accept` method will only be invoked by routers, and therefore it is guaranteed that the `accept` method will always receive non-null messages.

Complex to Simple Filter

One reason to implement a filter class is to condense multiple filters into one single class. An example of this is the `ExceptionTypeFilter`, which is meant to filter for messages whose payload is an exception. This is the equivalent of having a `PayloadTypeFilter` for exception messages.

Using an airline ticketing example, if a booking is being made by a frequent flyer member who has enough miles on this trip alone to qualify for a free upgrade, we would want to point that out to him. This means we need to filter for messages that have not been finalized yet (are unpaid and therefore still booking requests), which are for passengers who are frequent flyer members and who have enough miles on this trip to qualify for free upgrades.

```
public class AutoUpgradeFilter implements Filter

private int threshold;

public boolean accept (MuleMessage message)
{
    if (message.getPayload() instanceOf
       (BookingRequest)) {
        BookingRequest aBooking =
        message.getPayload();
    }
    return (aBooking.FrequentFlyer != null) ||
       (aBooking.FlyerMiles >= threshold);
}
```

In the preceding code, you can see a new filter class characterized by the fact that it implements the Filter interface. A private integer property called threshold, which will be configured at design time, allows different thresholds to be set. (The getter and setter methods are not shown here.)

The accept method extracts the payload of the message and returns true only if the FrequentFlyer field of the booking request is not null and if the FlyerMiles field of the booking request is larger than or equal to the threshold specified. The filter can then be reused for situations where we need to filter for different FrequentFlyer mile amounts.

Now let's look at the Mule configuration for our filter:

```
<service name="UpgradeService">
    <inbound>
        <vm:inbound-endpoint address="Bookings"/>
        <selective-consumer-router>
            <custom-filter class=
            "com.ricstonairways.filters.AutoUpgradeFilter">
                <spring:property name="threshold"
                  value="1500"/>
                </spring:property>
            </custom-filter>
        </selective-consumer-router>
    </inbound>
    <component class="com.ricstonairways.Upgrade"/>
</service>
```

In the preceding configuration, the inbound selective consumer router uses a custom filter that refers to our previous example, and which is set to have a threshold of 1500. All bookings read off the VM endpoint called Bookings will therefore be passed to the upgrade service provided that the passenger is a frequent flyer member and also has chosen a ticket that generates enough miles for a free upgrade.

The properties for the class are set using the Spring namespace. The custom filter is defined in the Mule schema and does not have a threshold attribute, so we cannot just add the item as an attribute in XML.

Creating a New Filter

Another example of a filter would be one that does something that the existing filters do not do, such as filter messages that contain attachments. This filter will only make sense if you read messages from SOAP or one of the e-mail transports (SMTP or POP3). However, you should avoid checking the transport directly as perhaps some new or improved transport in the future will support attachments; your filter should only look for the existence of attachments.

The filter criteria could use the `getAttachmentNames` method to see if an empty set is returned and return `true` or `false` based upon that. No additional parameters are required as there is nothing else that can be configured.

The filter class in this case is very simple; all it needs to do is match the result of the `getAttachmentNames()` method with an empty set.

```
public class HasAttachmentsFilter implements Filter

public boolean accept (MuleMessage message)
{
    return message.getAttachmentNames() == null;
}
```

Building a Router

All the routing patterns available in the Enterprise Integration Patterns[8] book are included inside Mule, and a wide range of message routers are there for you to use within your Mule applications. There are cases when you may need to tweak a pattern slightly so that it fits your architecture. This section shows how you can customize or combine routing patterns to achieve these aims.

Overview

Routers control how messages are sent or received by service components. Inbound routers control how messages are received from an endpoint and passed to a service component, while outbound routers control how

---

[8] "Enterprise Integration Patterns: Designing, Building, and Deploying Messaging Solutions" by Gregory Hohpe, Bobby Woolf `http://www.enterpriseintegrationpatterns.com/`.

messages dispatched by the service component are sent via one or more endpoints. The routers don't work with the messages directly; they operate on a `MuleEvent` that contains the `MuleMessage` together with other information (such as the endpoint) relevant to the context of the current message. Some additional methods are available to manipulate the current message.

Inbound routers can return an array of one or more Mule events to the service component. This would happen if a single message needs to be split into multiple ones or if the router is maintaining a list of messages (for instance if it is a resequencer router). It can also return a null message to show that the service has nothing to process. An aggregator router, for example, would return null when it receives individual messages, but will return a single message when it has the complete item.

Outbound routers can return the resulting message if the message flow is synchronous or will return null if the flow is asynchronous. The message may be processed in any number of ways depending on the actual routing logic encoded into the router.

MuleEvent Methods

The `MuleEvent` represents any data event occurring within the current Mule environment. It also contains the following methods to let you further manipulate the event and inspect the current message:

- `getEndpoint` will return the endpoint associated with this event.

- `isSynchronous` will indicate whether the event flow is synchronous.

- `isStopFurtherProcessing` checks to see if this message flow is meant to be continued or if it is being disposed of. You can set this manually by using the `setStopFurtherProcessing` method.

- `getMessage` will return the current message. This is a `MuleMessage` object.

- `getMessageAsBytes` will return the message as a byte array.

- `getMessageAsString` will return the message as a string. It will use the default encoding to perform the conversion.

- `transformMessage` will return the message in its transformed state. This will use the transformers configured on the endpoint.

- `transformMessageToBytes` will first transform the message and then convert it into a byte array.

- `transformMessageToString` will first transform the message and then convert it into a string. It will use the default encoding to do this.

Inbound Routers

The Inbound Router interface defines these basic functions for an inbound router:

- `isMatch` determines whether the current event should be handled by this router, usually by using filters. This method returns a boolean value that indicates whether the message should be accepted.

- `process` returns a null value or an array of Mule events.

All core inbound routers inherit from the `SelectiveConsumer` router, which implements the `InboundRouter` interface and adds the following properties:

- `filter` is a private property that contains the filter condition, if any. The filter can be set and retrieved using the getter and setter commands.

- `transformFirst` is another private property that defaults to `true` and indicates if the router should operate on the transformed message or not.

There are two further abstract inbound router classes that derive from the `SelectiveConsumer` router:

- `AbstractEventAggregator` knows how to aggregate a series of messages into a single message.

- `AbstractEventResequencer` knows how to receive a series of messages, resequence them, and forward them on.

Outbound Routers

The Outbound Router interface defines these basic functions for an outbound router:

- `setEndpoints` allows a number of endpoints to be set for this router. There are similar helper methods called `getEndpoints ()`, `addEndpoints()`, and `removeEndpoints()`.

- `setReplyTo` is an endpoint that will receive all responses. Other Mule routers will then use this property to send replies back.

- `setTransactionConfig` sets the configured transaction values.

- `isDynamicEndpoints` indicates whether this router expects configured endpoints or if it will build them up dynamically from the message payload or properties.

- `isMatch` determines whether the current event should be handled by this router, usually by using filters. This method returns a boolean value that indicates whether the message should be accepted.

- `route` is the method that routes the message. It will return null if the message flow is asynchronous and will return the `MuleMessage` if not.

All core outbound routers inherit from the `FilteringOutboundRouter`, which implements the `OutboundRouter` interface and adds the `filter` property—a property that contains the filter condition, if any. The filter can be set and retrieved using the getter and setter commands.

There are two additional abstract outbound router classes that derive from the `FilteringOutboundRouter` class:

- `AbstractMessageSplitter` knows how to split a message into multiple parts.

- `AbstractRecipientList` knows how to dispatch a single message to multiple recipients over the same transport.

Extending a Router

Extending an existing router means that we need to extend the routing mechanism. Note that this is different from extending the selection mechanism, since we can merely write a new filter for that. In this case, we need to extend or tweak one of the routing patterns to match our architecture.

Taking the Idempotent pattern as an example, the default mechanism uses the unique ID that a transport encodes within a `MuleMessage` to determine if the message has been processed or not. In our airline case, we want to use this pattern to make sure that a passenger does not try to make multiple bookings for himself. We could use a combination of the passenger name and the credit card number to enforce this pattern.

An Idempotent Router

We can start off by extending the `IdempotentReceiver` class that rejects messages if they have been processed. The ancestor class takes care of the necessary behavior for us—including maintaining and persisting a list of group IDs—but we need to override the mechanism to determine the ID for a given message. This is achieved using the `getIdForEvent()` method, which needs to be overridden to retrieve the `PassengerDetails` class from our `MuleMessage` and then create a new ID based on the passenger name and credit card number.

The `getIdForEvent()` method needs to return the group identifier for the current message as shown here:

```
{
  MuleMessage obj = event.getMessage();
  if (obj.getPayload() == null)
  {
    return null;
  }
  if (obj.getPayload() instanceof PassengerFlightQuery)
  {
    PassengerFlightQuery details =
      (PassengerFlightQuery) obj.getPayload();
    return details.getPassengerName() +";"
      +details.getCreditCardNumber();
  } else {
    return super.getIdForEvent (event);
  }
}
```

The method receives the `MuleEvent` that contains information about the entire message flow including the `MuleMessage`. If there is no payload, then we can return null as the ID and let the ancestor's rules for handling null values take over. If not null, we need to ensure that the payload really is a `PassengerFlightQuery` message. If it is, we can typecast the payload and extract the relevant information from it to return a valid ID. If it is not, then we can delegate responsibility to the ancestor for generating an ID.

Finally, here is the configuration for our router:

```
<inbound>
  <vm:inbound-endpoint path="FlightQuery"/>
  <custom-inbound-router class="com.ricstonairways.
      routers.SingleBookingPerPassengerRouter">
    <!- Custom filter? -->
  </custom-inbound-router>
</inbound>
```

For simplicity's sake, we have only displayed the inbound router collection here and not the details for the full service. As you can see, all details are neatly contained within code and nothing is exposed through configuration.

Don't forget that since all inbound routers inherit from the
`SelectiveConsumer` router, we can also add a filter to the configuration
should we want to.

Summary

Transformations may be application specific, and these must usually be
created as they are not available inside Mule. While you can choose to use
transformation on the bus or include transformation as a service in its own
right, Mule does not impose a restriction on you and you can use either
one.

The Transformer interface is what you should implement if you want to
create a raw transformer, but it makes sense to use the
`AbstractTransformer` class in the first place.

Filtering, on the other hand, offers the ability in Mule to choose whether to
send a message to a service component or not (or to an endpoint or not).
The Filter interface needs to be implemented; it allows for a single method
that will return `true` if the message matches the filter, or `false` if the
message does not. This operation will normally work on the complete
`MuleMessage`, that is, you can filter on any `MuleMessage` property or on
any property in the payload.

You will need to build your own filters either to combine multiple filters
into one simple class or to provide filtering support if none already exists.
If filtering is not the sort of routing pattern you want to extend or enhance,
the next section will explain how you can create new routers of your own.

In the last section, we saw how a routing pattern can be extended and how
this is different from extending filtering. Routers operate by manipulating
`MuleEvent` objects, which contain the `MuleMessage` and a set of methods
to manipulate the `MuleMessage`.

All core inbound and outbound routers inherit from the Filtering routing pattern—the `SelectiveConsumer` or the `FilteringOutboundRouter`. In either case, an in-depth knowledge of the routing patterns and how they're implemented inside Mule lets you pick the right one for your situation.

Chapter 8: Resilient Mule Applications

Any Mule application must be able to handle exceptional situations that can occur from time to time. This chapter will cover how you can manage and work with such exceptional situations.

Error Handling and Recovery

Error handling and recovery comes in various shapes and sizes and greatly depends on your application's needs. Developers can employ several techniques to handle exceptions.

One way is to log the error message with the appropriate information. Additionally, rather than merely sending the error to a log file, it could also be copied or sent to an alternative destination. This technique assumes that errors merely need to be flagged and that someone or something that can deal with errors is monitoring the destination. Even if the error will be handled automatically, logging the error is always useful when tracing a history of faults within a system.

Another method involves automatic troubleshooting, which implies that there is a planned solution for a predictable error condition. If such a condition can be coded and placed on the ESB, an application can sort out its own errors. Because such solutions would be precisely defined, the solution would not be appropriate if an exception varies slightly from what is expected.

Routing patterns involve applying one of the numerous exception routing patterns that are available to handle exceptions. Either of the previous two points—error logging or automatic troubleshooting—can be used within routing patterns.

Mule's Exception Strategy Classes

Mule has an abstract class, `org.mule.AbstractExceptionListener`, which is the basis for every exception strategy. This class has several methods that are of use, including those shown here:

- `rollbackTransaction()` is called to roll back the current transaction when an exception is received.

- `handleLifecycleException()` handles all exceptions thrown during an object's lifecycle, such as initializing, destroying, and so forth.

- `handleMessagingException()` handles exceptions thrown during normal message processing.

- `handleRoutingException()` handles exceptions thrown during message routing.

- `handleStandardException()` handles any other type of exception.

- `routeException()` routes the exception message to a given endpoint.

Mule's default exception strategy, `org.mule.DefaultExceptionStrategy`, grabs the exception, logs it into the default logger, and routes it to an alternative endpoint. There is also an exception strategy for services, called `org.mule.service.DefaultServiceExceptionStrategy`, which inherits from the `DefaultExceptionStrategy` but also knows which service raised the exception.

Configuring Exception Strategies

The `DefaultServiceExceptionStrategy` is configured on a model within the Mule configuration and has one attribute, `enableNotifications` which indicates whether Mule system notifications should be raised. By default this is set to `true`.

The `DefaultServiceExceptionStrategy` class has the following child elements:

- `commit-transaction` lets you specify a comma-separated list of wildcard patterns that Mule will match against the name of the exception. If the exception name matches, the transaction will not be rolled back.

- `rollback-transaction` lets you specify a comma-separated list of wildcard patterns that Mule will match against the name of the exception. If the exception name matches, the transaction will be rolled back.

- `outbound-endpoint` is the endpoint that the exception message will be routed to.

All exception strategies have these attributes and child elements. If you create your own strategy you will need to use the `<custom-exception-strategy>` element that has its own class attribute which should refer to your class.

Flexible Exception Strategies

What is rather flexible about Mule's exception-handling mechanism (illustrated in Figure 8-1) is that there is a distinction between exceptions related to the business or routing logic, and exceptions raised due to faults within the underlying technology.

- **Service exceptions** occur within your application's business logic. Because all business components are contained within a Mule model, an exception strategy can be placed on the model and used by all components that it hosts. It is important to note that these exception strategies will catch and handle any exceptions raised by the service, including any raised in the inbound or outbound routers.

- **Transport exceptions** relate to the connectors and are different from business exceptions because they can be handled differently. They may also need to be routed differently. The technologies are all represented in connectors, so you can add exception strategies for any connector defined inside your Mule configuration. If there is a technology exception, you will not be able to read or write to this sort of endpoint; Mule considers this a fatal condition.

Figure 8-1. Flexible Exception Strategies

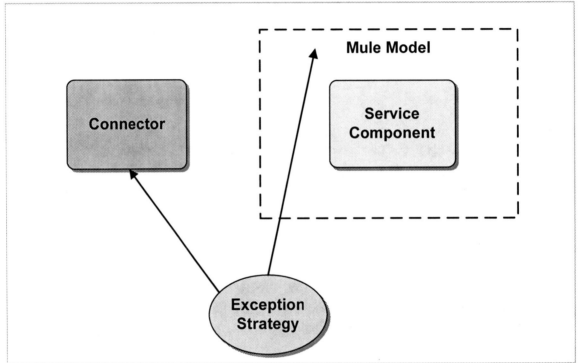

Service Exception Strategies

Service exception strategies need to handle errors that occur within the business logic. This could be some kind of logical error but is more likely to be an error within the business process. Think about a passenger with a valid airline ticket whose record isn't in the system. He cannot be checked in but his ticket is authentic, so what should be done?

This exception strategy will handle all exceptions that are raised at any point in the message flow, that is, in the inbound flow stage, the component flow stage, or the outbound flow stage. As you can see in the example that follows, the `DefaultServiceExceptionStrategy` can be configured on a model before all the services or within a single service after the outbound router collection:

```
<model name="myModel">
   <default-service-exception-strategy>
      <outbound-endpoint address="jms://Error.queue"/>
   </default-service-exception-strategy>
   ...
   <service name="anyService">

      ...
      <default-service-exception-strategy>
        <outbound-endpoint address="jms://Other.error"/>
      </default-service-exception-strategy>
   </service>

</model>
```

Any exception that occurs within any of these services will be routed to the JMS endpoint called `Error.queue`, but exceptions raised within the service called `anyService` will be routed to the JMS endpoint called `other.error`.

Transport Exceptions

Transport exceptions are thrown by transports or transformers when there is a problem with the underlying technology, for example with reading data off an endpoint or with writing data to an endpoint. These exceptions are fatal exceptions; if there is a problem receiving or dispatching from/to a transport, the whole message flow fails. A service exception would only be raised for one message—all others will continue as normal.

Note   You should make sure to take care of these exceptions; otherwise an unexpected exception will halt your Mule server.

You can configure the exception strategy to use the
`DefaultConnectorExceptionStrategy` class inside the connector, as
shown here:

```
<vm:connector name="myConnector">
    <default-connector-exception-strategy>
     <outbound-endpoint address="stdio://OUT"/>
   </default-connector-exception-strategy>
</vm:connector>
```

Exception Strategies—Create Your Own

If you want to create your own exception strategies, you can extend the
`DefaultExceptionStrategy` to perform your own routing and error
handling. This implements all the abstract methods from the
`AbstractExceptionListener` class, so it is a better place to start from.

You can choose to override any of the standard methods that handle the
different exception types.

Note   Your code must contain the exception, should never itself throw
an exception, and that fatal exceptions must also be managed.

Routing Patterns—Exception Router

One of the patterns from the EIP book is an exception-based router. This
router is configured with two or more endpoints and will route along the
first one that does not fail. In Mule it is implemented as `<exception-
based-router>` and can be configured as shown here:

```
<outbound-router>
  <exception-based-router">
     <tcp:outbound-endpoint
            host="10.192.111.10" port="8080"/>
     <tcp:outbound-endpoint
```

```
          host="10.192.111.11" port="8081"/>
      <jms:outbound-endpoint queue="pendingItems"/>
    </exception-based-router>
  </outbound-router>
```

In this case, Mule will attempt to route the message along the first endpoint. If it cannot, any exception strategies associated with this transport will be activated, but if a `FatalConnectException` is raised, it will try routing it on the second endpoint. This is repeated until all of the endpoints have been tried, at which point an `org.mule.api.routing.RoutingException` is thrown.

Transactions in Mule

While we can cater for unexpected situations, we know that if an error occurs during a process, any data from queues or databases may need to be restored to leave the system in a consistent state. Transactions let us do this; we will see what sorts of transactions we can use in Mule in this section.

A transaction is generally described as a unit of interaction that guarantees the integrity of a data source. This can be a database, therefore referred to as a JDBC transaction, or it can be a queue, as in the case of a JMS transaction.

The lifecycle of a transaction inside an ESB consists of keeping track of the message flows that are meant to participate in the transaction once it has started. If any errors occur the entire transaction must be rolled back. If there are no errors all changes should be committed.

The key to all this is determining where the transaction boundaries lie, that is, where a transaction should (and can) start and where it should end.

Single vs. XA Transactions

Mule supports single-resource transactions and therefore natively supports JDBC and JMS transactions. Because the VM transport also has transaction support, you can use this to simulate transactionality while you are modeling your application. Apart from this, Mule also supports XA transactions, which allow you to start a transaction in one transport and end it in another.

Mule's transaction framework is independent of the underlying technology, so single-resource and multiple-resource transactions are all treated in the same way, making configuration easier.

The endpoints need to be configured for transactionality since data is consumed from, or sent to, the underlying technology on/from endpoints. In each case we can configure whether a new transaction needs to start on an endpoint or whether the endpoint should join an existing one.

The Transaction Manager

Every Mule application needs to have a transaction manager that controls the transactions within Mule. This is defined within `<transaction-manager>` XML elements and should be declared before the connectors. The `transaction-manager` element has two attributes:

- `name`, which defaults to `transactionManager`, but which you can optionally set to any name.

- `factory`, which is used to refer to a specific transaction class.

If Mule is deployed on an application server (for example JBoss or WebSphere), you can, and in some cases, must, use the transaction manager provided by the application server. Mule provides a series of transaction-manager classes that are specific to each application server, as listed here:

- `<websphere-transaction-manager/>`

- `<jboss-transaction-manager/>`

- `<weblogic-transaction-manager/>`

- `<jrun-transaction-manager/>`

- `<resin-transaction-manager/>`

If Mule is not deployed on an application server you can use the default JBoss transaction manager (formerly called Arjuna) by including a declaration for it before the Mule model.

```
<jboss-transaction-manager/>
```

Transactional Endpoints

Endpoints can be made transactional by adding the appropriate `<transaction>` element to an `<endpoint>` tag. Valid transaction elements are as follows:

- `<jms:transaction>` refers to a JMS transaction.

- `<jdbc:transaction>` refers to a JDBC transaction.

- `<jms-client-ack-transaction>` is a wrapper around the message acknowledgment feature of JMS. Rollback is not supported, but it is useful when consuming items off a JMS destination.

- `<vm:transaction>` refers to a VM transaction.

These items have two attributes:

- `action` tells Mule what to do for each Mule message received. This instruction can be any of the following:

  - NONE: Never participate in a transaction.

  - ALWAYS_BEGIN: Always start a new transaction at this point. If a transaction already exists and is in progress, raise an exception.

- BEGIN_OR_JOIN: Join a transaction if one has started; otherwise create a new one.

- ALWAYS_JOIN: Always join a transaction, as one should have started. If there is no transaction, raise an exception.

- JOIN_IF_POSSIBLE: If a transaction is in progress, join it; otherwise continue as normal.

- timeout refers to the length of time, in milliseconds, that Mule should wait before rolling back the transaction if it isn't complete.

Examples

The examples that follow demonstrate how transactions are configured on endpoints. This first example is a JMS transaction:

```
<jms:inbound-endpoint queue="test.In">
    <jms:transaction action="ALWAYS_BEGIN"
        timeout="60000"/>
</jms:inbound-endpoint>
```

Every message read from the test.In JMS queue will be contained inside a single-resource transaction that will time out after 60 seconds unless it is committed.

In this second example every record retrieved by the getOrder SQL query will join an existing JDBC transaction:

```
<jdbc:inbound-endpoint queryKey="getOrder?type=2">
        <jdbc:transaction action="ALWAYS_JOIN"/>
</jdbc:inbound-endpoint>
```

Normally, transactions are configured on the inbound endpoint, since this is the first point where data is consumed from queues or databases. This consumption would need to be rolled back to maintain consistency. A service's outbound endpoints will automatically join the current transaction if there is one, so there is no need to set any transaction elements. Multiple outbound endpoints, for example in a MessageSplitter outbound router, will all participate in the transaction if they can. However, if your transaction boundary starts on an outbound endpoint, the configuration shown previously can be used there instead.

Caution   If a message is inside a transacted message flow and it gets directed to a nontransactional endpoint, surprise timeouts may occur since there may not be a valid response even if there was no error.

XA Transactions

XA transactions allow single transactions to span multiple resources. In Mule this means JMS and/or JDBC and/or VM. The configuration is similar to the previous one, but instead of using a JMS transaction element you need to use the JMS XA transaction element (or a JDBC XA transaction element or a VM XA transaction element). You need to ensure that your transaction manager is XA-enabled; otherwise this will cause run-time problems.

If you compare the following configuration example to the example in the previous section, you will see how similar the configurations are:

```
<inbound-endpoint address="jms://my.queue">
   <jms:xa-transaction action="ALWAYS_BEGIN"
          timeout="60000"/>
</inbound-endpoint>
```

At the time of writing, one of the proposed changes for the next version of Mule (2.1) is to move the `xa-transaction` element into the `mule` namespace.

Poison Messages

If you read a message from a queue within a transaction and an exception occurs, the whole transaction is rolled back and the message is placed back on to the queue. This behavior is as expected, but what if the message itself caused the exception? In this case it will cause the exception again as soon as it is re-read and processed. Such a message is referred to as a "poison message."

Since exceptions can be caused by a number of issues, not just poison messages, you can configure how many times you want this rollback-and-read pattern to be invoked by adjusting the value of the maxRedelivery attribute on the JMS connector. It defaults to zero, so at the first exception the message will not be re-read by the connector.

Connection Strategies

Connection strategies provide the means, when writing or configuring transports, to specify the action Mule should take when message delivery fails due to an issue with the transport/connector. When defining connection strategies you can specify properties or attributes that determine factors such as the number of times Mule should attempt to reconnect, the time interval between retries before giving up, and the action to take on failure.

Connection strategies are included as a standard feature in the Mule 1.x Community Edition; however, they have been not been implemented in the Mule 2.0 Community Edition and will appear as a feature available only in the Enterprise Edition.

Summary

In this chapter we've looked at ways to make your Mule applications more resilient.

First we saw how exceptions can be handled in Mule as well as routed to a destination for further processing. This is preferable to letting Mule fail when it encounters exceptions that it does not know how to handle.

Exception strategies can handle different types of exceptions differently, so there is no need to have one single mechanism to cater for all possibilities. The basic behavior inside the `DefaultExceptionStrategy` is to route the exception message to an endpoint and log the exception into the log file. The `DefaultServiceExceptionStrategy` does the same thing, but is also aware of which service raised the exception. All of these strategies can be configured within a model to cater for all services within the model, or within a connector to cater for technology exceptions. Should the default behavior not suffice, you can extend the default classes and build your own.

Transactions, on the other hand, are there to guarantee integrity of the data that's being used. Mule supports JMS and JDBC transactions and also allows the use of XA transactions to span multiple resources. Additionally, VM can be included in transactions so that you can model transactions before rolling out the live technologies.

Mule needs to be configured with a transaction manager that will manage the transaction; each endpoint will then need a transaction element to indicate how it should participate within a transaction. This is done on the inbound side as outbound endpoints will automatically participate in an existing transaction.

Copyright

Mule 2: A Developer's Guide to ESB and Integration Platform

© 2008 by Ricston, Ltd., Peter Delia, and Antoine Borg

Technical Reviewer: Ross Mason

ISBN-13 (electronic): 978-1-4302-0982-9

ISBN-13 (paperback): 978-1-4302-0981-2

Trademarked names may appear in this book. Rather than use a trademark symbol with every occurrence of a trademarked name, we use the names only in an editorial fashion and to the benefit of the trademark owner, with no intention of infringement of the trademark.

Distributed to the book trade in the United States by Springer-Verlag New York, Inc., 233 Spring Street, 6th Floor, New York, NY 10013, and outside the United States by Springer-Verlag GmbH & Co. KG, Tiergartenstr. 17, 69112 Heidelberg, Germany.

In the United States: phone 1-800-SPRINGER, fax 201-348-4505, e-mail orders@springer-ny.com, or visit http://www.springer-ny.com. Outside the United States: fax +49 6221 345229, e-mail orders@springer.de, or visit http://www.springer.de.

For information on translations, please contact Apress directly at 2855 Telegraph Ave, Suite 600, Berkeley, CA 94705. Phone 510-549-5930, fax 510-549-5939, e-mail info@apress.com, or visit http://www.apress.com.

Services for Mule & Open Source

Ricston training for Mule is delivered to users around the globe through our training partners. We specialize in developing training programmes and content; we also have extensive direct experience providing consulting, technical support and training for Mule.

Whether you are looking for a public course in your area or want an on-site course tailored for your team; we can meet your requirements…

To find public training in your region, visit; www.ricston.com/courses/, select the desired course and reserve your place via the website.

To request private/on-site training, send an email to; info@ricston.com and we will design a custom-built solution for you.